W9-CLL-179

SPOTLIGHT

NORTH CAROLINA COAST

SARAH BRYAN

Contents

NORTH CAROLINA COAST

THE OUTER BANKS

The Outer Banks are like a great seine net set along the northeastern corner of North Carolina, holding the Sounds and inner coast apart from the open ocean, yet shimmying obligingly with the forces of water and wind. The Outer Banks can be—and on many occasions have been—profoundly transformed by a single storm. A powerful hurricane can fill in a centuries-old inlet in one night, and open a new channel wherever it pleases. As recently as 2003, Hatteras Island was cut in half—by Hurricane Isabel—though the channel has since been artificially filled. This evanescent landscape poses challenges to the life that it supports, and creates adaptable and hardy plants, animals, and people.

The Sounds are often overlooked by travelers, but they are an enormously important part of the state and region. Collectively known as the Albemarle-Pamlico Estuary, North Carolina's Sounds—Albemarle, Pamlico, Core, Croatan, Roanoke, and Currituck—form the second-largest estuarine system in the country (second only to the Chesapeake Bay). They cover nearly 3,000 square miles, and drain more than 30,000. The diverse marine and terrestrial environments shelter crucial plant and animal communities, as well as estuarine systems that are essential to the environmental health of the whole region, and to the Atlantic Ocean.

Sheltered from the Atlantic, the Inner Banks are much more accommodating, ecologically speaking, than the Outer Banks. Wetlands along the Sounds invite migratory birds by the hundreds of thousands to shelter and rest, while pocosins (a special kind of bog found in

HIGHLIGHTS

◖ Fort Raleigh National Historic Site:
Here at the site of the Lost Colony, the myste-
rious first chapter of English settlement in the
New World unfolded in the 1580s (page 19).

◖ Ocracoke Island: On this remote island,
you'll find a historic village that is the home of
one of America's most unique local communities, as well as some serious water sports and
walking opportunities (page 28).

◖ The Great Dismal Swamp: This natural
wonder straddling the Virginia/Carolina line
is an amazing place for canoeing or kayaking,
bird-watching, and sightseeing (page 31).

◖ Somerset Place Historic Site: The
graceful architecture and exotic setting of this
early plantation contrast with the tragic history of its slavery days (page 37).

◖ Pettigrew State Park: Lake Phelps, the
centerpiece of Pettigrew State Park, is an attractive enigma, a body of shallow water and
deep history (page 38).

**◖ Mattamuskeet National Wildlife
Refuge:** The landmark lodge on Lake
Mattamuskeet towers over a dramatic waterscape that attracts migratory birds by the tens
of thousands (page 41).

LOOK FOR ◖ TO FIND RECOMMENDED SIGHTS, ACTIVITIES, DINING, AND LODGING.

the region) and maritime forests have nurtured
a great multitude of life for eons. Here is where
North Carolina's oldest towns—Bath, New
Bern, and Edenton—set down roots, from
which the rest of the state grew and bloomed.
In Washington County, 4,000-year-old canoes
pulled out of Lake Phelps testify to the region's
unplumbed depths of history.

PLANNING YOUR TIME

The reasons for visiting the coast in spring and
summer are obvious: the beach, the restaurants
and attractions that are only open in-season,
and the warm-weather festivals. But coastal
North Carolina is beautiful four seasons of the

year, and for many people fall and winter are
favorite times to visit.

Around the time that the beach-bound traffic starts to thin out a little, towards the end of
summer, eastern North Carolina's other busy
season begins. Slow-moving trucks carry loads
of loose tobacco leaves, bound from the field to
the barn for curing. Stray yellow-green, wilted
leaves litter the roadsides, blown off the trucks.
On Saturdays in the early autumn, the air is
heavy in pockets with the smoke of yard fires,
as folks clear out their summer gardens and
the hot-weather overgrowth on their properties, and prepare for the cool-weather plant-
ing season. Collard patches are put in, often

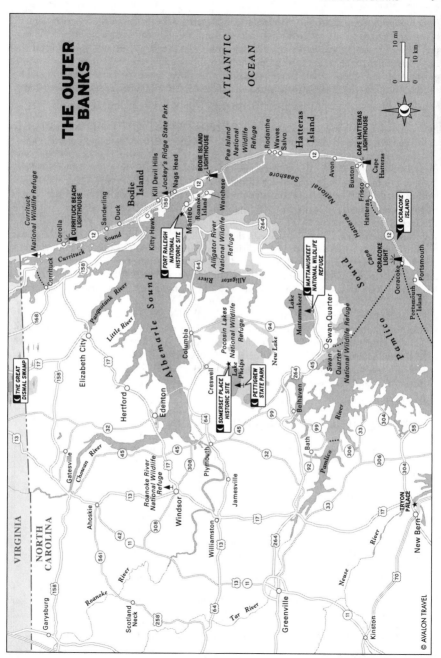

THE OUTER BANKS

© AVALON TRAVEL

right alongside houses. At their sweetest after being touched by frost, collards are a favorite among fanciers of greens who prefer that musty mildness to the acrid twang of mustard greens. Cotton comes ripe late in the year. As the bolls begin to ripen, farm workers strip off the plants' leaves, until only the flowering bolls remain atop the stalks. The stark beauty of a field of ripe cotton is a mesmerizing sight.

Fall and winter are wonderful times for canoeing and kayaking on eastern North Carolina's rivers, creeks, and swamps. The weather is often more than mild enough for comfort, and the landscape and wildlife are not so obscured by tropical verdancy as they are in the spring and summer. A word of caution: Don't assume that you won't encounter alligators or snakes in the winter. They're never far away, and even a brief warm spell can have them out of their dens and looking for trouble. Wear snake boots if you have them, don't wade or swim in fresh water, and keep a lookout for gators' snouts along the surface of the water. Oftentimes all that's visible of an alligator are his nostrils and the little bony ridges of his brow. Spend enough time around gators, and you'll become accustomed to scanning the water before putting in.

Autumn, of course, is peak hurricane season.

Dazzlingly beautiful in their ferocity, hurricanes are an unforgettable experience for anyone who has lived through one. For all the thrill, though, one should go to great pains to avoid them. Evacuation orders must always be obeyed, because hurricanes really are deadly, and highly unpredictable.

INFORMATION AND SERVICES

The **Aycock Brown Welcome Center** at Kitty Hawk (U.S. 158, MP 1.5, 877/629/4386, www .outerbanks.org, 9 A.M.–5 P.M. daily Dec.–Feb., 9 A.M.–5:30 P.M. daily Mar.–May and Sept.–Nov., 9 A.M.–6 P.M. daily June–Aug.), Outer Banks Welcome Center at Manteo, and Cape Hatteras National Seashore Visitors Center on Ocracoke, are all clearinghouses for regional travel information. The **Outer Banks Visitors Bureau** (www.outerbanks.org) can be reached directly at 877/629-4386.

Major **hospitals** are located in Nags Head, Windsor, Washington, Edenton, Ahoskie, and Elizabeth City. On Ocracoke, only accessible by air or water, non-emergency medical situations can be addressed by **Ocracoke Health Center** (305 Back Rd., 252/928-1511, after hours 252/928-7425). (Note that 911 works on Ocracoke, as everywhere else.)

PRONUNCIATION PRIMER

North Carolina is full of oddly pronounced place names, and this farthest northeast corner is a good place to pause for our first lesson in talking like a native. The Outer Banks are a garland of peculiar names, as well as names that look straightforward but are in fact pronounced in unexpectedly quirky ways. If you make reference publicly to the town of Corolla, and pronounce it like the Toyota model, you'll be recognized right away as someone "from off." It's pronounced "Ker-AH-luh." Similarly, Bodie Island, site of the stripy lighthouse, is pronounced "Body," as in one's earthly shell. That same pattern of pronouncing Os as Ahs, as in "stick out your tongue and say 'ah,'" is repeated farther down the coast at Chicamacomico, which comes out "Chick-uh-muh-CAH-

muh-co." But just to keep you on your toes, the rule doesn't apply to Ocracoke, which is pronounced like the Southern vegetable and Southern drink: "Okra-coke."

Farther south along the banks is the town of Rodanthe, which has an elongated last syllable, "Ro-DANTH-ee." On Roanoke Island, Manteo calls out for a Spanish emphasis, but is in fact front-loaded, like so many Carolina words and names. It's pronounced "MAN-tee-oh," or "MANNY-oh." Next door is the town of Wanchese. This sounds like a pallid dairy product, "WAN-cheese." Inland, the Cashie River is pronounced "Cuh-SHY," Bertie County is "Ber-TEE," and Chowan County is "Chuh-WON." Think the names around here are singular? Just wait until you get to the mountains.

Nags Head and Vicinity

The Outer Banks of North Carolina, unlike many barrier islands elsewhere in the world, are not attached to anchoring coral reefs. Instead, the Banks are a long sandbar, constantly eroding and amassing, slip-sliding into new configurations with every storm. The wind is the invisible player in this process, the man behind the curtain giving orders to the water and the

sand. The enormous dune known as Jockey's Ridge was a landmark to early mariners, visible from miles out to sea.

According to legend, Nags Head was a place of sinister peril to those seafaring men. Islanders, it's said, would walk a nag or mule, carrying a lantern around its neck, slowly back and forth along the beach, trying to lure ships into the shallows where they might founder or wreck, making their cargo easy pickings for the land pirates.

It was the relentless wind at Kill Devil Hill that attracted the Wright brothers to North Carolina. It also brought the Rogallos, pioneer hang-glider inventors. Today, it brings thousands of enthusiasts every year, hang-gliders and parasailers, kite-boarders and kite-flyers. Add to these pursuits sailing, surfing, kayaking, hiking, birding, and, of course, beach-going, and the northern Outer Banks are perhaps North Carolina's most promising region for outdoor adventurers. Several reserves encompass large swaths of the unique ecological environments of the Banks, though increasingly the shifting sands are given over to the gamble of human development.

SIGHTS
Wright Brothers National Memorial

Though they are remembered for a 12-second flight on a December morning in 1903, Wilbur and Orville Wright actually spent more than three years coming and going between their home in Dayton, Ohio, and Kitty Hawk, North Carolina. As they tested their gliders on Kill Devil Hill, the tallest sand dune on the Outer Banks, the Wright brothers were assisted by many Bankers. The locals fed and housed them, built hangars, and assisted with countless practicalities that helped make the brothers' experiment a success. On the morning of December 17, 1903, several local men were present to help that famous first powered flight get off the ground. John Daniels, a

Map

To Duck, Corolla, and Currituck National Wildlife Refuge

WRIGHT MEMORIAL BRIDGE

RUNDOWN CAFÉ

AYCOCK BROWN WELCOME CENTER

NAGS HEAD AND VICINITY

Currituck Sound

ATLANTIC OCEAN

Kitty Hawk

BEACH HAVEN MOTEL
MILE POST 4

W. KITTY HAWK RD.

Kitty Hawk Woods

BALDVIEW B&B

Kitty Hawk Bay

CHIP'S WINE AND BEER MARKET
MILE POST 6

Kill Devil Hills

COLINGTON CREEK INN

WRIGHT BROTHERS NATIONAL MEMORIAL
MILE POST 8

COLINGTON RD.

Colington

CYPRESS HOUSE INN

OUTER BANKS BREWING STATION

COLONY IV BY THE SEA
MILE POST 9

Albemarle Sound

Nags Head Woods Ecological Preserve

MILE POST 10

KELLY'S OUTER BANKS RESTAURANTS

Nags Head

LUCKY 12 TAVERN

0   1 mi
0   1 km

US 158/S. CROATAN HWY (THE BYPASS)

NC 12/VIRGINIA DARE TR (BEACH ROAD)

MILE POST 12

KILL DEVIL GRILL AND FOOD DUDES KITCHEN

Jockey's Ridge State Park

OUTER BANKS DIVE CENTER

© AVALON TRAVEL

lifesaver from a nearby station, took the iconic photograph of the airplane lifting off. It was the first and only photograph he ever made. He was later quoted in a newspaper as saying of the flight, "I didn't think it amounted to much." But it did, and that flight is honored at the Wright Brothers National Memorial (Milepost 7.5 of Hwy. 158, Kill Devil Hills, 252/441-7430, www.nps.gov/wrbr, park open daily year-round, visitors center 9 A.M.–6 P.M. daily June–Aug., 9 A.M.–5 P.M. daily Sept.–May). At the visitors center, replica gliders are on display, along with artifacts from the original gliders and changing displays sponsored by NASA. You can also tour the reconstructed living quarters and flight hangar, and, of course, climb Kill Devil Hill to get a glimpse of what that first aviator saw.

Jockey's Ridge State Park

Jockey's Ridge State Park (Carolista Dr. off Milepost 12 of Hwy. 158, Nags Head, 252/441-7132, www.jockeysridgestatepark.com, 8 A.M.–6 P.M. daily Nov.–Feb., 8 A.M.–7 P.M. daily Mar. and Oct., 8 A.M.–8 P.M. daily Apr.,

May, and Sept., 8 A.M.–9 P.M. daily June–Aug.) contains 420 acres of a strange and amazing environment, the largest active sand dune system in the eastern United States. Ever-changing, this ocean-side desert is maintained by the constant action of the northeast and southwest winds. Visitors can walk on and among the dunes. It's a famously great place to fly kites, go sand-boarding, and hang-glide. (Hang-gliding requires a valid USHGA rating and a permit supplied by the park office.)

Nags Head Woods Ecological Preserve

Bordering Jockey's Ridge is another unique natural area, the Nature Conservancy's Nags Head Woods Ecological Preserve (701 W. Ocean Acres Dr., about 1 mile from Milepost 9.5 of Hwy. 158, 252/441-2525, www.nature .org/wherewework/northamerica/states/north-carolina/preserves/art5618.html, dawn–dusk daily year-round). Nags Head Woods is over 1,000 acres of deciduous maritime forest, dunes, wetlands, and inter-dune ponds. More than 50 species of birds nest here in season,

© SARAH BRYAN

visitors atop the giant dune at Jockey's Ridge State Park

NAGS HEAD IN 1849

My first impressions of Nag's Head were very favorable... when we hove in sight of the harbor, in the gray of the morning, and saw the sun rise over Nag's Head, making still more than the usual contrast between the white sand-hills and the dark, beautiful green of its clusters of oak, when we discerned the neat white cottages among the trees, the smoke curling lazily from the low chimneys, the fishing-boats and other small craft darting to and fro, the carts plying between the shore and the dwellings, the loiterers who were eager to know who and how many had arrived...

– Gregory Seaworthy,
Nags Head, or, Two Months Among "the Bankers" (1849)

including ruby-throated hummingbirds, green herons, and red-shouldered hawks, and it is also home to a host of other animals and unusual plants. Maps to the public trails are available at the visitors center.

Kitty Hawk Woods

Slightly smaller but no less important is the Nature Conservancy's Kitty Hawk Woods (south of Hwy. 158 at Kitty Hawk, trail access from Woods Rd. and Birch Ln., off Treasure St., 252/261-8891, www.nature.org/wherewework/northamerica/states/northcarolina/preserves/art5611.html, dawn–dusk daily year-round). These maritime forests harbor the unusual species of flora and fauna of the maritime swale ecosystem, a swampy forest sheltered between coastal ridges. Kitty Hawk Woods is open to the public for hiking and birding, and can be explored from the water as well. A canoe and kayak put-in is next to the parking lot of **Kitty Hawk Kayaks** (6150 N. Croatan Rd./Hwy. 158, 252/261-0145, www.khkss.com).

© SARAH BRYAN

walking paths through wetlands and woods at the Nags Head Woods Ecological Preserve

INNOCENCE EXCEPTED

In 1728, William Byrd of Westover, a Virginia planter and man of letters, took part in an expedition to mark the dividing line between his home state and North Carolina. In his *Histories of the Dividing Line*, he detailed his adventures in the marshy wilds of Carolina, including a March 1728 encounter with a pair of castaways at Currituck Inlet.

While we continued here, we were told that on the south shore, not far from the inlet, dwelt a marooner, that modestly called himself a hermit, though he forfeited that name by suffering a wanton female to cohabit with him.

His habitation was a bower, covered with bark after the Indian fashion, which in that mild situation protected him
pretty well from the weather. Like the ravens, he neither plowed nor sowed, but subsisted chiefly upon oysters, which his handmaid made a shift to gather from the adjacent rocks. Sometimes, too, for change of diet, he sent her to drive up the neighbor's cows, to moisten their mouths with a little milk. But as for raiment, he depended mostly upon his length of beard, and she upon her length of hair, part of which she brought decently forward, and the rest dangled behind quite down to her rump, like one of Herodotus's East Indian pygmies.

Thus did these wretches live in a dirty state of nature, and were mere Adamites, innocence only excepted.

Currituck Heritage Park

The shore of Currituck Sound is an unexpected place to find the art deco home of a 1920s industrial magnate. The **Whalehead Club** (1100 Club Rd., off of Milepost 11 from Route 12, 252/453-9040, www.whaleheadclub.com, visitors center open 11 A.M.–5 P.M. daily, standard tours 9 A.M.–4 P.M. daily, specialty tours require 24 hours advance notice, $5–15) was built as a summer cottage by Edward Collings Knight Jr., an industrialist whose fortune was in railroads and sugar. This beautifully simple yellow house—only a "cottage" by the standards of someone like Knight—sits on a peaceful spit of land that catches the breeze off the sound. It's the centerpiece of Currituck Heritage Park, where visitors can picnic, wade, or launch from the boat ramp, in addition to touring the house.

Next to the Whalehead Club is the **Outer Banks Center for Wildlife Education** (Currituck Heritage Park, Corolla, 252/453-0221, www.ncwildlife.org, 9 A.M.–5 P.M. daily, free). With exhibits focusing on the native birds, fish, and other creatures of Currituck Sound, the Center also has a huge collection

Currituck Beach Lighthouse

of antique decoys—an important folk tradition of the Carolina coast—and offers many special nature and art programs throughout the year. (Check the website for a program calendar.)

The 1875 **Currituck Beach Lighthouse** (Currituck Heritage Park, 252/453-4939, 10 A.M.–6 P.M. daily Easter–October, 10 A.M.–5 P.M. daily in November, closed December–Easter, closed in very rough weather, $7, children under 7 free) stands on the other side of the Center for Wildlife Education. It is one of the few historic lighthouses that visitors can climb. The 214-step spiral staircase leads to the huge Fresnel lens, and a panoramic view of Currituck Sound.

Corolla Wild Horse Museum

In the town of Corolla, the circa-1900 Corolla Schoolhouse has been transformed into a museum honoring the wild horses of the Outer Banks. The Corolla Wild Horse Museum (1126 Old Schoolhouse Ln., Corolla, 252/453-8002, 10 A.M.–4 P.M. Mon.–Sat. in the summer, off-season hours vary, free) tells of the history of the herd, which once roamed all over Corolla, but now live in a preserve north of the town.

ENTERTAINMENT AND EVENTS

Chip's Wine and Beer Market (Milepost 6, Croatan Hwy./Route 158, Kill Devil Hills, 252/449-8229, www.chipswinemarket.com) is, in addition to what the name suggests, the home of **Outer Banks Wine University.** In at least two classes a week, Chip himself and other instructors host wine and beer tastings with an educational as well as gustatory bent.

Nightlife

The **Outer Banks Brewing Station** (Milepost 8.5, Croatan Hwy./Hwy. 158, Kill Devil Hills, 252/449-2739, www.obbrewing.com) was founded in the early 1990s by a group of friends who met in the Peace Corps. The brewery/restaurant they built here was designed and constructed by Outer Bankers, modeled on the design of the old life-saving stations so important in the region's history. The pub serves several very gourmet homebrews at $4.50 for a pint, and $6 for four five-ounce samplers. They've also got a nice lunch and supper menu, with elaborate entrées as well as the requisite pub fare.

Bacu Grill (Outer Banks Mall, Milepost 14 on Hwy. 158, Nags Head, 252/480-1892), a Cuban-fusion restaurant, features live jazz and blues music, and serves good beer, wine, and snacks into the wee hours of the morning. **Kelly's Outer Banks Restaurant and Tavern** (Milepost 10.5 on Hwy. 158, Nags Head, 252/441-4116, www.kellysrestaurant.com, 4:30 P.M.–midnight Sun.–Thurs., 4:30 P.M.–2 A.M. Fri.–Sat.) is also a good bet for live music, and has a long wine list with some lovely vintages. **Lucky 12 Tavern** (3308 S. Virginia Dare Tr., Nags Head, 252/255-5825, www.lucky12tavern.com, 11:30 A.M.–2 A.M. daily) is a traditional sports bar with TVs, foosball, and New York–style pizza.

SPORTS AND RECREATION
Kayaking

Coastal Kayak (make reservations at North Beach Outfitters, 1240 Duck Rd., Duck, 252/261-6262, www.coastalkayak.org) offer tours throughout the northern Outer Banks, including guided trips through the Alligator River National Wildlife Refuge and the Pea Island National Wildlife Refuge, as well as the Pine Island Audubon Sanctuary and Kitty Hawk Woods. Tours last from two and a half to three and a half hours, and cost between $35 and $50.

Diving

The **Outer Banks Dive Center** (3917 S. Croatan Hwy., 252/449-8349, www.obxdive.com) offers instruction, and guided tours of wrecks off the coast of the Outer Banks. Guided wreck dives are only available from April through November. All levels of divers are welcome.

Hiking and Touring

The **Currituck Banks National Estuarine Preserve** (Hwy. 12, 252/261-8891, www.nc

coastalreserve.net) protects nearly 1,000 acres of woods and water extending into Currituck Sound. A third-of-a-mile boardwalk runs from the parking lot to the Sound, and a primitive trail runs from the parking lot 1.5 miles through the maritime forest.

Back Country Outfitters and Guides (107-C Corolla Light Town Center, Corolla, 252/453-0877, http://outerbankstours.com) leads a variety of tours in the Corolla region, including Segway beach tours, wild horse–watching trips, kayaking, and other off-road tours.

Surfing

The North Carolina coast has a strong surfing culture—not to mention strong waves—making this a top destination for experienced surfers and those who would like to learn.

Island Revolution Surf Co. and Skate (252/453-9484, www.islandrevolution.com, group lessons $60/person, private $75, must be older than 8 and a good swimmer) offers private and one-on-one surfing lessons as well as board rentals. So do **Ocean Atlantic Rentals** (Corolla Light Town Center, 252/453-2440, www.oar-nc.com, $50/person group lessons, $75 private, $120 couples, must know how to swim, locations also in Duck, Nags Head, and Avon), and **Corolla Surf Shop** (several locations, 252/453-9283, www.corollasurfshop.com, 9 years old and up).

Online resources for Outer Banks surfing include the website of the Outer Banks District of the Eastern Surfing Association (http://outerbanks.surfesa.org), www.wrightcoastsurf.com, www.obxsurfinfo.com, and www.surfkdh.com.

Kayaking

The Outer Banks combines two very different possible kayaking experiences—the challenge of ocean kayaking, and the leisurely drifting zones of the salt marshes and back creeks. **Kitty Hawk Sports** (798 Sunset Blvd., 252/453-6900, www.kittyhawksports.com) is an old and established outdoors outfitter that leads kayaking and other expeditions. Another good bet is **Kitty Hawk Kayaks** (6150 N. Croatan Hwy., Kitty Hawk, 866/702-5061, www.khkss.com), which teaches kayaking and canoeing, rents equipment for paddling and surfing, and leads tours (including overnight expeditions) through gorgeous waterways in pristine habitats, in cooperation with the Nature Conservancy.

Kitty Hawk Kites (877/359-8447, www.kittyhawk.com), which *National Geographic Adventure* magazine calls one of the "Best Adventure Travel Companies on Earth," has locations throughout the Outer Banks, including at Corolla. They too teach and lead hanggliding, parasailing, jet skiing, kiteboarding, kayaking, and lots more ways to ride the wind and water.

ACCOMMODATIONS

The █ **First Colony Inn** (6720 Virginia Dare Trail, Nags Head, 800-368/9390, www.firstcolonyinn.com, $69–299/night depending on season) is a wonderful 1932 beachfront hotel. This regional landmark has won historic preservation and landscaping awards for its 1988 renovation, which involved moving the entire building, in three pieces, three miles south of its original location. The pretty and luxurious rooms are surprisingly affordable.

The **Sanderling Resort and Spa** (1461 Duck Rd., near Duck, 877/650-4812, www.thesanderling.com, $130–450) is a full-sized, conventional resort, with three lodges, a spa, three restaurants (on- and off-site) including the **Lifesaving Station,** housed in an 1899 maritime rescue station, and various sports and recreational rental options.

Bed-and-breakfasts include the sound-front **Cypress Moon Inn** (1206 Harbor Ct., Kitty Hawk, 877/905-5060, www.cypressmooninn.com, no guests under 18), with three pretty guest rooms. The **Baldview B&B** (3805 Elijah Baum Rd., Kitty Hawk, 252/255-2829, www.baldview.com, $125–200, no children or pets) is a modern residence located on a beautiful property along the sound, with four nicely appointed guestrooms and a carriage house. The **Colington Creek Inn** (1293 Colington Rd., Kill Devil Hills, 252/449-4124, www.colingtoncreekinn.com,

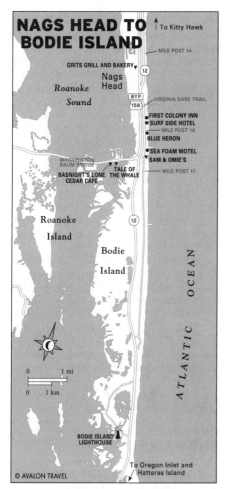

In Kitty Hawk and Nags Head, you'll find an abundance of motels, from chains to classic 1950s mom-and-pops. The **Surf Side Hotel** (6701 Virginia Dare Tr., Nags Head, www.surfsideobx.com, 800/552-7873, from $55 out of season, from $165 in-season) is a favorite for simple and comfortable accommodations, with standard rooms and efficiencies in a location right on the dunes. All rooms at the **Blue Heron** (6811 Virginia Dare Tr., Nags Head, 252/441-7447, www.blueheronnc.com, from $50 out of season, from $130 in-season) face the ocean. The Blue Heron has a heated indoor pool as a consolation on rainy days. Super-affordable is the **Sea Foam Motel** (7111 Virginia Dare Tr., Nags Head, 252/441-7320, www.outer-banks.nc.us/seafoammotel/index.htm, from $62 out of season, from $110 in-season), an old-timer with a lot of retro appeal. Other good choices in the area include the **Colony IV by the Sea** (405 S. Virginia Tr., Kill Devil Hills, 252/441-5581, www.motelbythesea.com, from $70 out of season, $68–163) and **Beach Haven Motel** (Ocean Rd. Milepost 4, Kitty Hawk, 888/559-0506, www.beachhavenmotel.com, from $65 out of season, from $105 in-season).

FOOD

Sam & Omie's (7728 S. Virginia Dare Trail, Nags Head, 252/441-7366, www.samandomies.net, 7 A.M.–10 P.M. daily March–mid-Dec.) was opened during the summer of 1937, a place for charter fishing customers and guides to catch a spot of breakfast before setting sail. It still serves breakfast, with lots of options in the eggs and hotcakes department, including a few specialties like crab and eggs Benedict. It also has a dinner menu starring seasonal steamed and fried oyster, Delmonico steaks, and barbecue.

Tale of the Whale (7575 S. Virginia Dare Tr., Nags Head, 252/441-7332, www.taleofthewhalenagshead.com, dinner entrées $15–50) sits at a beautiful location, at the very edge of the water with a pier jutting into Roanoke Sound. There's outdoor music from a pier-side gazebo and a dining room with such a great view of the water that it feels like the inside of a ship—but the real draw is the incredibly

$168–198 depending on season, no children or pets) is a large outfit with a great view of the sound and the creek it's named for.

The **Cypress House Inn** (Milepost 8, Beach Rd., Kill Devil Hills 800/554-2764, www.cypresshouseinn.com, $99–199, depending on season) is a very traditional coastal Carolina-style house, built in the 1940s, with an easy walk to the beach. Its hurricane shutters and cypress-paneled rooms will give you a taste of Outer Banks life in the days before the motels and resorts.

THE OUTER BANKS

extensive menu of seafood, steak, and pasta specials. They also have an imaginative cocktail menu.

Grits Grill and Bakery (5000 S. Croatan Hwy., Nags Head, 252/449-2888, 6 A.M.– 3 P.M. daily) is a favorite for breakfast, famous for its biscuits, Krispy Kreme donuts, eggs, and, of course, grits.

The (**Blue Point** (1240 Duck Rd., Duck, 252/261-8090, www.goodfoodgoodwine.com, $20–35) has a nouveau Southern menu, with staples like catfish and trout done up in the most creative ways. Among the specialties, fresh Carolina shrimp is presented on "barley risotto," with broccolini, wine-soaked raisins, and lemon arugula pesto. Try the key lime pie with raspberry sauce, Kentucky bourbon pecan pie, or seasonal fruit cobblers. After-dinner drinks (among them espresso martinis and special dessert wines) complement an amazing wine list, which is, if anything, even more impressive than the menu. There are at least a dozen vintages in almost every category (prices ranging from $7/glass to $250/bottle), and several top-notch single-malts and small-batch bourbons. The Blue Point also occupies an amazing building, a custom-built waterside home with diner-style seating, an open kitchen with a counter and bar stools running its length, checkered floors, and a big screen porch. Reservations can be made online as well as by phone up to a month in advance, and are very necessary: Peak hours in season are booked two and three weeks in advance, while even winter weekends are usually booked solid several days before.

Owens' Restaurant (Milepost 16.5 on Beach Rd., Nags Head, 252/441-7309, www .owensrestaurant.com) has been in operation at Nags Head for more than 60 years, and in addition to their good seafood menu, visitors enjoy looking over the owners' collection of historical artifacts from Outer Banks maritime life.

New as of 2009, **Blue Moon Beach Grill** (4104 S. Virginia Dare Tr., Nags Head, 252/261-BLUE, www.bluemoonbeachgrill .com, 11:30 A.M.–9 P.M. daily, $12–25) is rapidly

becoming a local favorite. Known for its seafood dishes, Blue Moon is also a popular place to grab a draft beer after work.

Tortuga's Lie (Milepost 11.5 on Hwy. 158 on Beach Rd., 252/441-7299, www.tortugas lie.com) has a good and varied menu specializing in seafood (some of it local) cooked in Caribbean-inspired dishes, with some good vegetarian options.

For casual and on-the-go chow options at Nags Head, try **Maxximuss Pizza** (5205 S. Croatan Hwy., Nags Head, 252/441-2377), which specializes in calzones, subs, and panini, in addition to pizza; **Yellow Submarine** (Milepost 14, Hwy. 158 Bypass, Nags Head, 252/441-3511), a super-casual subs and pizza shop; or **Majik Beanz** (4104 S. Virginia Dare Tr., Nags Head, 252/255-2700) for coffee and shakes.

The **Kill Devil Grill** (2008 S. Virginia Dare Trail, 252/449-8181, $13–20) serves hearty meals for brunch, lunch, and dinner. Entrées include excellent seafood and steaks. Vegetarians will find limited options, but meat eaters will be well satisfied. **Food Dudes Kitchen** (1216 S. Virginia Dare Tr., Kill Devil Hills, 252/441-7994, $10–17) has great seafood, wraps, and sandwiches. **Rundown Café** (5218 N. Virginia Dare Tr., Kitty Hawk, 252/255-0026, $10–15) is a popular local eatery with affordable Caribbean-influenced fare.

GETTING THERE AND AROUND

The closest major airport to this region is the **Norfolk International Airport** (2200 Norview Ave., 757/857-3351, www.norfolkairport.com), approximately an hour from the northern Outer Banks. **Raleigh-Durham International Airport** (2600 W. Terminal Blvd., 919/840-2123, www.rdu.com) is 3–5 hours from most Outer Banks destinations.

Only two bridges exist between the mainland and the northern Outer Banks. U.S. 64/264 crosses over Roanoke Island to Whalebone, just south of Nags Head. Not too far north of there, Highway 158 crosses from Point Harbor to Southern Shores. Highway 12 is the main road all along the northern Outer Banks.

Roanoke Island

Roanoke Island was the site of the Lost Colony, one of the strangest mysteries in all of American history. Its sheltered location— nestled between the Albemarle, Roanoke, and Croatan Sounds, and protected from the ocean by Bodie Island—made Roanoke Island a welcoming spot for that party of ocean-weary Englishmen in the 1580s. Unhappily, they lacked the foresight to make one of the bed-and-breakfast inns in Manteo or Wanchese their home base, so that after a hard day of fort-building they could relax with a hot bath and free wireless Internet. Instead they cast their lots in the wilderness, and what befell them may never be known.

At the northern end of Roanoke Island is the town of Manteo and the Fort Raleigh National Historic Site. This is where most of the tourist attractions and visitor services are concentrated. At the southern end is Wanchese, where some of Dare County's oldest families carry on their ancestral trades of fishing and boatbuilding.

◖ FORT RALEIGH NATIONAL HISTORIC SITE

Fort Raleigh National Historic Site (1401 National Park Dr., Manteo, 252/473-5772, www.nps.gov/fora, park open sunup–sundown daily year-round except Christmas Day, visitors center 9 A.M.–5 P.M. daily Sept.–May, 9 A.M.–6 P.M. daily June–Aug., admission to park free, admission charged to Elizabethan Gardens and "The Lost Colony") comprises much of the original site of this first English settlement in the New World. Some of the earthworks associated with the original 1580s fort remain and have been preserved. The visitors center displays some of the artifacts discovered during this restoration effort. Two nature trails in the park explore the island's natural landscape and the location of a Civil War battle.

Within the National Historic Site, two of Manteo's most famous attractions operate autonomously. About 60 years ago, Manteo's **Elizabethan Gardens** (Fort Raleigh National Historic Site, 252/473-3234,

the lush Elizabethan Gardens within the Fort Raleigh National Historic Site

© CINDY HAGGERTY / 123RF.COM

www.elizabethangardens.org, hours vary by season and day of the week, $8 adult, $5 ages 5–17) was conceived by the Garden Club of North Carolina as a memorial to the settlers of Roanoke Island. Much of the beautifully landscaped park recreates the horticulture of the colonists' native England in the 16th century. Many special nooks throughout the gardens hold treasures, such as: an ancient live oak believed to have been standing in the colonists' time; a Shakespearean herb garden; and a 19th-century statue of Virginia Dare that lay underwater off the coast of Spain for two years, was salvaged from a fire in Massachusetts, and upon her arrival in North Carolina in the 1920s was considered so racy that for decades she was tossed back and forth like a hot potato all across the state.

Also within the park boundaries is the Waterside Theater. North Carolina has a long history of outdoor drama celebrating regional heritage, and the best known of the many productions across the state is Roanoke Island's **"The Lost Colony"** (Fort Raleigh National Historic Site, Roanoke, 252/473-3414, www .thelostcolony.org, $18–24 adults, $15 seniors, $12 children 11 and under, $20 "producer's circle" seats). Chapel Hill playwright Paul Green was commissioned to write the drama in 1937, to celebrate the 350th anniversary of Virginia Dare's birth. What was expected to be a single-season production has returned almost every year for more than 70 years, interrupted only occasionally for emergencies such as prowling German U-boats.

OTHER SIGHTS

The **North Carolina Maritime Museum,** whose mother ship is located in Beaufort, operates a branch here on Roanoke Island (104 Fernando St., Manteo, 252/475-1750, www.obxmaritime .org, hours vary seasonally, free). In addition to the many traditional Outer Banks working watercraft on display, the museum holds boat-building and -handling courses at its George Washington Creef Boathouse. Visitors not enrolled in classes can still come in and watch traditional boat builders at work in the shop.

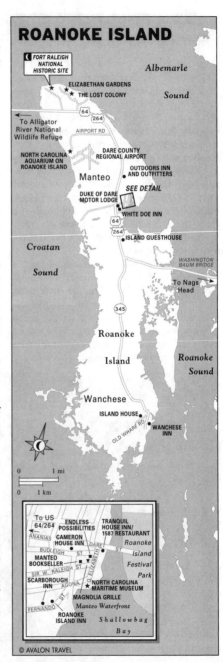

The **North Carolina Aquarium on Roanoke Island** (374 Airport Rd., 3 miles north of Manteo, 866/332-3475, www.ncaquariums .com/roanoke-island, 9 A.M.–5 P.M. daily, $8 adults, $7 seniors, $6 ages 6–17, under 5 free) is one of three state aquariums here on the North Carolina coast. It's a great place to visit and see all sorts of marine fauna: sharks and other, less ferocious, fish, crustaceans, octopuses, turtles, and more. Like its sister aquariums, it's also a research station where marine biologists track and work to conserve the native creatures of the coast.

Roanoke Island Festival Park (1 Festival Park, Manteo, 252/475-1500, www.roanoke island.com, 9 A.M.–5 P.M. daily Feb. 19– Apr. 1, 9 A.M.–6 P.M. daily Apr. 1–Nov. 1, 9 A.M.–5 P.M. daily Nov. 1–Dec. 31, closed Jan. 1–Feb. 19, $8 adults, $5 ages 6–17, under 5 free) is a state-operated living history site. The highlight is the *Elizabeth II,* a reconstruction of a 16th-century ship like the ones that brought Sir Walter Raleigh's men to the New World. There are also a museum, a reconstructed settlement site, and several other places where costumed interpreters will tell you about daily life in the Roanoke colony.

SPORTS AND RECREATION

The **Outdoors Inn and Outfitters** (406 Uppowoc Ave., Manteo, 252/473-1356, www .theoutdoorsinn.com) offers scuba instruction, beach dives, dive boat charters, and swimming lessons. Kayak tours include wildlife and dolphin watching, birding, saltmarsh, and photography tours.

TOURS

The **Downeast Rover** (sails from Manteo waterfront, 252/473-4866, www.downeast rover.com, daytime cruises adults $30, children 2–12 $15, sunset cruises $40) is a reproduction 19th-century 55-foot schooner that sails from Manteo on daytime and sunset cruises. Cruises last two hours and depart three times a day, at 11 A.M., 2 P.M., and at sunset. To see the Outer Banks from the air, your options include a World War II biplane or a closed-cockpit Cessna through **Fly the Outer Banks** (410 Airport Rd., Manteo, 252/202/7433, $38–98), or a biplane through **Barrier Island Aviation** (407 Airport Rd., 252/473-4247, www.barrier islandaviation.com, $40–150).

ENTERTAINMENT AND EVENTS

Outer Banks Epicurean Tours (252/305-0952, www.outerbanksepicurean.com) are a wonderful way to dine royally, while learning about the rich culinary traditions of this region and how the Banks' natural history creates this unique cuisine. The four-hour tours, which start at $95/person (not including the price of any alcohol you wish to order), give a teeth-on introduction to the native fish and shellfish of the area and the heritage of the people who harvest them, to bees and beekeeping, local wineries and microbreweries, coastal barbecue, indigenous and colonial cuisines, and many other topics.

SHOPPING

Manteo Booksellers (105 Sir Walter Raleigh St., 252/473-1221 or 866/473-1222, www .manteobooksellers.com, 10 A.M.–6 P.M. daily) is a great independent bookstore, specializing in Outer Banks history and nature, but with a wide selection for all tastes.

Endless Possibilities (105 Budleigh St., 252/475-1575, www.ragweavers.com, 10 A.M.–5 P.M. Mon.–Sat.) is an unusual sort of a shop. Here you can buy purses, boas, rugs, and other adornments of home and body, made from recycled second-hand clothes. All the profits go to support the Outer Banks Hotline Crisis Intervention and Prevention Center, a regional help line for victims of rape and domestic violence, and an HIV/AIDS information center. And if you happen to be in Manteo long enough, you can even take lessons here to learn how to weave.

ACCOMMODATIONS

The ◖ White Doe Inn (319 Sir Walter Raleigh St., 800/473-6091, www.whitedoeinn.com, from $175 out of season, from approx. $350

THE LOST COLONY

On July 4, 1584, an expedition of Englishmen commissioned by Sir Walter Raleigh dropped anchor near Hatteras Island. Within a couple of days, local Native Americans were coming and going from the English ships, scoping out trade goods and making proffers of Southern hospitality. They got on famously, and when the Englishmen crossed the ocean again to bring tidings of the land they had found to Raleigh and the Queen, two Indian men, Manteo and Wanchese, came along as guests. It seems that Wanchese was somewhat taciturn and found London to be no great shakes, but Manteo got a kick out of everything he saw, and decided that Englishmen were all right.

In 1585, a new expedition set out for Roanoke, this time intending to settle in earnest. When they reached the Pamlico Sound, their bad luck began. Most of their store of food was soaked and ruined when seawater breached the ship, so from the moment they arrived on shore they were dependent on the mercy of the Indians. Manteo and Wanchese went to Roanoke chief Wingina to discuss the Englishmen's plight. Wanchese, who was, it would turn out, a man of superior insight, tried to convince Wingina to withhold help. But Manteo pled the colonists' case convincingly, and the Englishmen were made welcome. Winter rolled around, and the colonists, having grown fat and happy on the Indians' food, were doing precious little to attain self-sufficiency. Then a silver cup disappeared from the Englishmen's compound. It was posited that the thief came from a nearby village, which was promptly burned to the ground. Worried about his own people, Wingina shuttered the soup kitchen, hoping the English would either starve or go away. Instead, they killed him. Three weeks later, an English supply ship arrived with reinforcements of men and material, but they found the colony deserted.

Yet another attempt was made, this time with whole families rather than gangs of rowdy single men. A young couple named Eleanor and Ananais Dare was expecting a child when they landed at Roanoke, and soon Virginia Dare was born, the first English child born in America. The Native American situation grew worse, though, and the Roanoke tribe, now under the leadership of Wanchese, were unwilling to aid a new wave of colonists. Manteo, still a friend, tried to enlist the help of his kinfolks, but they were facing lean times as well. John White, leader of the expedition and grandfather of Virginia Dare, lit out on what he planned would be a fast voyage back to England for supplies and food. Through no fault of his own, it was three years before he was able to come back. When he did, he found no sign of the settlers, except "CRO" carved on a tree, and "CROATOAN" on a rail.

Thus began 400 years of wonderment and speculation that will probably never be resolved. Some believe that the English were killed, some that they were captured and sold into slavery among tribes farther inland. Several communities in the South of uncertain or mixed racial heritage believe themselves to be descendants of the lost colonists (and some evidence suggests that this might in fact be possible). The answers may never be found, and for the foreseeable future the mystery will still hang heavily over Roanoke Island and its two towns: Manteo and Wanchese.

in-season) is one of North Carolina's premier inns. The 1910 Queen Anne is the largest house on the island, and is on the National Register of Historic Places. Rooms are exquisitely furnished in turn-of-the-century finery. Guests enjoy a four-course breakfast, evening sherry, espresso and cappuccino any time, and a 24-hour wine cellar. Spa services are available on-site, and you need only step out to the lawn to play croquet or bocce.

The **Roanoke Island Inn** (305 Fernando St., 877/473-5511, www.roanokeislandinn.com, $150–200) has been in the present owner's family since the 1860s. It's a beautiful old place, with a big porch that overlooks the marsh. They also rent a single cottage on a private island, five minutes away by boat, and a nice cypress-shingled bungalow in town. Another top hotel in Manteo is the **Tranquil House Inn** (405 Queen Elizabeth Ave., 800/458-7069, www.1587.com, $109–239). It's in a beautiful location (hard not to be, on this island), and downstairs is one of the best restaurants in town, 1587. The **Scarborough Inn** (524 Hwy. 64, 252/473-3979, www.scarborough-inn.com, $75–125 depending on season) is a small hotel with 12 rooms and great rates. It's the sort of old-time hotel that's hard to find these days.

The **Cameron House Inn** (300 Budleigh St., Manteo, 800/279-8178, http://cameron-houseinn.com, $130–210) is a cozy 1919 Arts and Crafts–style bungalow. All of the indoor rooms are furnished in a lovely and understated Craftsman style, but the nicest room in the house is the porch, which has an outdoor fireplace, fans, and flowery trellises.

The **Island Guesthouse** (706 Hwy. 64, 252/473-2434, www.theislandmotel.com, rooms from $60 out of season, from $85 in-season, cottages from $125 out of season, from $200 in-season, pets welcome with fee) offers simple and comfortable accommodations in its guest house, with two double beds, air conditioning, and cable TV in each room. They also rent out three tiny, cute cottages. Another affordable option is the **Duke of Dare Motor Lodge** (100 S. U.S. 64, 252/473-2175, from $42 in-season). It's a 1960s motel, not at all fancy, but a fine choice when you need an inexpensive place to lay your head.

Over in Wanchese, the **Wanchese Inn** (85 Jovers Ln., Wanchese, 252/475-1166, www.wancheseinn.com, from $69 out of season, from $129 in-season) is a simple and inexpensive bed-and-breakfast. It's a nice Victorian house (with modern rooms), and there is a boat slip and available on-site parking for a boat and trailer. The **Island House** (104 Old Wharf Rd., 866/473-5619, www.islandhouse-bb.com, $85–175) was built in the early 1900s for a local Coast Guardsman, with wood cut from the property and nails forged on-site. It's very comfortable and quiet, and a big country breakfast is served every day.

© SARAH BRYAN

Wanchese, on Roanoke Island, is a quiet fishing town that is far less developed than neighboring Manteo.

FOOD

Located in the Tranquil House Inn, with a great view of Shallowbag Bay, **€ 1587** (405 Queen Elizabeth Ave., 252/473-1587, www.1587.com, dinner entrées $18–29) is widely regarded as one of the best restaurants in this part of the state. The menu is of hearty chops and seafood, with local ingredients in season, and a full vegetarian menu is also available upon request. The wine list is a mile long.

Basnight's Lone Cedar Café (Nags Head–Manteo Causeway, 252/441-5405, www.lonecedarcafe.com, 5 P.M.–closing Mon.–Wed., 11:30 A.M.–3 P.M. and 5 P.M.–closing Thurs.–Sat., 11 A.M.–closing Sun., closed in winter, lunch entrées $6–18, dinner entrées $18–31) is a water-view bistro that specializes in local food—oysters from Hyde and Dare Counties, fresh-caught local fish, and North Carolina chicken, pork, and vegetables. It's one of the most popular restaurants on the Outer Banks, and they don't take reservations, so be sure to arrive early. The full bar is open until midnight.

The **Full Moon Café** (208 Queen Elizabeth St., 252/473-6666, www.thefullmooncafe.com, 11:30 A.M.–9 P.M. daily in season, call for off-season hours, $10–30) is simple and affordable, specializing in quesadillas and enchiladas, wraps, sandwiches, a variety of seafood and chicken bakes, and quiches. Despite the seemingly conventional selection, the food here is so good that the Full Moon has received glowing reviews from the *Washington Post* and the *New York Post*—quite a feat for a little café in Manteo.

The **Magnolia Grille** (408 Queen Elizabeth St., 252/475-9787, www.roanokeisland.net/lp/magnoliagrille, 7 A.M.–4 P.M. Sun. and Mon., 7 A.M.–8 P.M. Tues.–Sat.) is a super-inexpensive place for all three meals of the day, and snacks in between. They've got a great selection of breakfast omelets, burgers, salads, soups, and deli sandwiches, with nothing costing more than $7.

GETTING THERE AND AROUND

Coming from the mainland, you'll reach the town of Mann's Harbor on the inland side of the Croatan Sound, and there you have two choices for crossing to Roanoke Island. If you take U.S. 64/264, to the north/left, you'll cross the sound to the north, arriving in Manteo. If you stay straight at Mann's Harbor you'll be on 64/264 Bypass, which crosses to the middle of the island, south of Manteo. Proceed until you get to the main intersection, where you can turn left onto 64/264 to go to Manteo, or right onto 345 towards Wanchese.

To reach Roanoke Island from the Outer Banks, take 158 or 12 to Whalebone Junction, south of Nags Head, and cross Roanoke Sound on the 64/264 bridge.

Cape Hatteras National Seashore

To many Americans, Cape Hatteras is probably familiar as a name often repeated during hurricane season. Hatteras protrudes farther to the southeast than any part of North America, a landmark to centuries of mariners, and a prime target for storms.

Cape Hatteras, the "Graveyard of the Atlantic," lies near Diamond Shoals, a treacherous zone of shifting sandbars that lies between the beach and the Gulf Stream. Two channels, Diamond Slough and Hatteras Slough, cross the shoals in deep enough water for a ship to navigate safely, but countless ships have missed their mark and gone down off Cape Hatteras. The 1837 wreck of the steamboat *Home* on the Shoals, which killed 90 passengers, led Congress to pass the Steamboat Act, which established the requirement of one life vest per passenger in all vessels.

In 2003, Hurricane Isabel inflicted tremendous damage, and even opened a new channel right across Hatteras Island, a 2,000-foot-wide

© NC DIVISION OF TOURISM

Cape Hatteras National Seashore

swash that was called Isabel Inlet. It separated the towns of Hatteras and Frisco, washing out a large portion of the highway that links the Outer Banks. For some weeks afterwards, Hatteras residents had to live as their fore-bears had, riding ferries to school and to the mainland. The inlet has since been filled in and Highway 12 reconnected, but Isabel Inlet's brief reign of inconvenience highlighted the vulnerability of life on the Outer Banks.

BODIE ISLAND

The 156-foot **Bodie Island Lighthouse** (6 mi. south of Whalebone Junction), whose huge Fresnel lens first beamed in 1872, was the third to guard this stretch of coast. The first light was built in the 1830s, but leaned like the Tower of Pisa. The next stood straight, but promised to be such a tempting target for the Yankee Navy during the Civil War that the Confederates blew it up themselves. (An unfortunate flock of geese nearly put the third lighthouse out of commission soon after its first lighting, when they collided with and

damaged the lens.) The lighthouse is not open to the public, but the keeper's house has been converted into a visitors center (252/441-5711, call for seasonal hours). This is also the starting point for self-guided nature trails to Roanoke Sound through the beautiful marshy landscape of Bodie Island.

The **Oregon Inlet Campground** (Hwy. 12, 877/444-6777, $20/night), operated by the National Park Service, offers camping behind the sand dunes, with cold showers, potable water, and restrooms.

HATTERAS ISLAND

Cape Hatteras makes a dramatic arch along the North Carolina coast, sheltering the Pamlico Sound from the ocean as if in a giant cradling arm. The cape itself is the point of the elbow, a totally exposed, vulnerable spit of land that's irresistible to hurricanes because it juts so far to the southeast. Along the Cape Hatteras National Seashore, Hatteras Island is just barely wide enough to support a series of small towns—Rodanthe, Waves, Salvo, Avon, Buxton, Frisco, and the village of Hatteras—and a great deal of dramatic scenery on all sides.

Sights

Lifesaving operations are an important part of North Carolina's maritime heritage. Corps of brave men occupied remote stations along the coast, ready at a moment's notice to risk— and sometimes to give—their lives to save foundering sailors in the relentlessly dangerous waters off the Outer Banks. In Rodanthe, the **Chicamacomico Life Saving Station** (Milepost 39.5 on Hwy. 12, Rodanthe, 252/987-1552, www.chicamacomico.net, noon–5 P.M. Mon.–Fri. mid-Apr.–Nov., $6, $5 under 17 and over 62 years old) preserves the original station building, a handsome, gray-shingled 1874 building, the 1911 building that replaced it—and which now houses a museum of fascinating artifacts from maritime rescue operations—and a complex of other buildings and exhibits depicting the lives of lifesavers and their families.

Cape Hatteras Lighthouse (near Buxton, 252/473-2111, www.nps.gov/caha/planyour visit, $7, $3.50 children and seniors, children smaller than 3'5" not permitted), at 208 feet tall, is the tallest brick lighthouse in the United States. It was built in 1870 to protect ships at sea from coming upon the Shoals unaware. It still stands on the cape, and it is open for climbing during the warm months. If you have a healthy heart, lungs, and knees, and are not claustrophobic, get your ticket and start climbing. The lighthouse is open daily from the third Friday in April–Columbus Day: 9 A.M.–4:30 P.M. in the spring and fall; 9 A.M.–5:30 P.M. early June–Labor Day. Tickets are required and are sold on the premises beginning at 8:15 A.M. Climbing tours run every ten minutes starting at 9 A.M.

Sports and Recreation

Pea Island National Wildlife Refuge (Hwy. 12, 10 mi. south of Nags Head, 252/987-2394, www.fws.gov/peaisland) occupies the northern reach of Hatteras Island. Much of the island is covered by ponds, making this an exceptional

© TERESA LEVITE / 123RF.COM

Cape Hatteras Lighthouse

place for watching migratory waterfowl. Two nature trails link some of the best bird-watching spots, and one, the half-mile North Pond Wildlife Trail, is fully wheelchair-accessible. Viewing and photography blinds are scattered along the trails for extended observation.

The Outer Banks owe their existence to the volatile action of the tides. The same forces that created this habitable sandbar also make this an incredible place for water sports. **Canadian Hole,** a spot in the sound between Avon and Buxton, is one of the most famous windsurfing and sail-boarding places in the world. (It goes without saying that it's also perfect for kite-flying.) The island is extraordinarily narrow here, so it's easy to tote your board from the sound side over to the ocean for a change of scene.

As with any sport, it's important to know your own skill level and choose activities accordingly. Beginners and experts alike, though, can benefit from the guidance of serious water sports instructors. **Real Kiteboarding**

(Cape Hatteras, 866/732-5548, www.realkite boarding.com) is the largest kiteboarding school in the world. They offer kiteboarding camps and classes in many aspects of the sport for all levels. **Outer Banks Kiting** (Avon, 252/305-6838, www.outerbankskiting.com) also teaches lessons and two-day camps, and carries boarders out on charter excursions to find the best spots.

There are all manner of exotic ways to tour Hatteras. **Equine Adventures** (252/995-4897, www.equineadventures.com) leads two-hour horseback tours through the maritime forests and along the beaches of Cape Hatteras. With **Hatteras Parasail** (Hatteras, 252/986-2627, www.hatterasparasail.com, $60 parasail ride, $35 kayak tour) you can ride 400 feet in the air over the coast, or even higher with **Burrus Flightseeing Tours** (Frisco, 252/986-2679, www.hatterasislandflightseeing.com, $35–62.50/person depending on flight and number of riders in party).

Accommodations

Among the lodging choices on Hatteras Island is the very fine **Inn on Pamlico Sound** (49684 Hwy. 12, Buxton, 252/995-7030 or 866/995-7030, www.innonpamlicosound.com, $120–320 depending on season). The inn is right on the sound, with a private dock and easy waterfront access. The dozen suites are sumptuous and relaxing, many with their own decks or private porches. Another good choice is the **Cape Hatteras Bed and Breakfast** (46223 Old Lighthouse Rd./Cape Point Way, Buxton, 800/252-3316, $119–159), which is only a few hundred feet from the ocean. Guests rave about the breakfasts.

Simpler motel accommodations include the clean, comfortable, and pet-friendly **Cape Pines Motel** (47497 Hwy. 12, Buxton, 866/456-9983, www.capepinesmotel.com, $49–159 depending on season, $20/pet); the **Outer Banks Motel** (47000 Hwy. 12, Buxton, 252/995-5601 or 800/995-1233, www.outerbanksmotel.com, $49–120 depending on season and style of accommodation), with both motel rooms and cottages; and the **Avon Motel** (Avon, 252/995-5774, www.avonmotel.com, $43–131

depending on season and style of accommodation, $10/pet), a pet-friendly motel that has been in business for more than 50 years.

CAMPING
Rodanthe Watersports and Campground (24170 Hwy. 12, 252/987-1431, www.watersportsandcampground.com) has a sound-front campground for tents and RVs under 25 feet, with water and electrical hookups and hot-water showers. Rates are $19.25 per night for two people, $4.75 for each additional adult, $3 for children and dogs, and an extra $4.75 per night for electrical hookup.

The Park Service operates two campgrounds in this stretch of the National Seashore. The **Frisco Campground** opens in early April, and **Cape Point Campground** at Buxton opens in late May (46700 Lighthouse Rd., Buxton, and 53415 Billy Mitchell Rd., Frisco, 877/444-6777, $20/night). At Frisco, one actually camps in the dunes, whereas at Cape Point, like the other NPS campgrounds here, the campsites are level and located behind the dunes. All have cold showers, bathrooms, and potable water. **Frisco Woods Campground** (Hwy. 12, Frisco, 800/948-3942, www.outer-banks.com/friscowoods, $30–90/night depending on accommodations and season) has a full spectrum of camping options, from no-utilities tent sites and RV sites with partial or full hookup to one- and two-bedroom cabins. The campground has wireless Internet access, hot showers, and a coin laundry.

Food
Though the **Restaurant at the Inn on Pamlico Sound** (Hwy. 12, Buxton, 252/995-7030, www.innonpamlicosound.com) is primarily for guests of the inn, if you call in advance you might be able to get a reservation for dinner even if you're staying elsewhere. The chef likes to use fresh-caught seafood, sometimes caught by the guests themselves earlier in the day. Vegetarian dishes and other special requests are gladly served.

For breakfast, try the **Gingerbread House** (52715 Hwy. 12, Frisco, 252/995-5204), which serves great baked goods made on the premises.

◖ OCRACOKE ISLAND

Sixteen miles long, Ocracoke Island comprises the southernmost reach of the Cape Hatteras National Seashore. The history of Ocracoke Island is, frankly, a little bit creepy. There's the remoteness, first of all. One of the most geographically isolated places in North Carolina, it's only accessible today by water and air. Regular ferry service didn't start until 1960, and it was only three years before that that Ocracokers had their first paved highway. In 1585, it was one of the first places in North America seen by Europeans, when the future Lost Colonists ran aground here. It may have been during the time they were waylaid at Ocracoke ("Wococon," they called it) that the ancestors of today's wild ponies first set hoof on the Outer Banks. Theirs was not the last shipwreck at Ocracoke, and in fact, flotsam and goods that would wash up from offshore

wrecks was one of the sources of sustenance for generations of Ocracokers.

In the early 18th century, Ocracoke was a favorite haunt of Edward Teach, better known as the pirate Blackbeard. He lived here at times, married his 14th wife here, and died here. Teach's Hole, a spot just off the island, is where a force hired by Virginia's Governor Spottswood finally cornered and killed him, dumping his decapitated body overboard (it's said to have swum around the ship seven times before going under), and sailing away with the trophy of his head on the bowsprit.

All of **Ocracoke Village,** near the southern end of the island, is on the National Register of Historic Places. While the historical sites of the island are highly distinctive, the most unique thing about the island and its people is the culture that has developed here over the centuries. Ocracokers have a "brogue" all their own, similar to those of other Outer Banks communities, but so distinctive that, in the unlikely event that there were two native Ocracokers

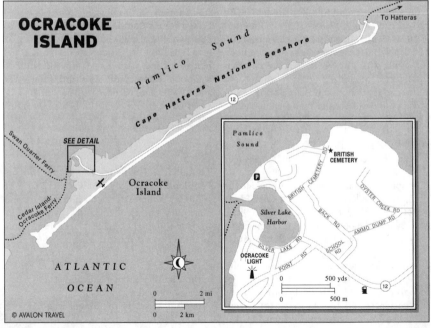

who didn't know each other already, and they happened to cross paths somewhere out in the world, they would recognize each other right away as neighbors (and probably cousins) by the cadences of their speech.

Ocracoke Lighthouse

A lighthouse has stood on Ocracoke since at least 1798, but due to constantly shifting sands, the inlet that it protected kept sneaking away. Barely 20 years after that first tower was built, almost a mile stretched between it and the water. The current Ocracoke Light (village of Ocracoke, 888/493-3826) was built in 1823, originally burning whale oil to power the beam. It is still in operation—the oldest operating light in North Carolina, and the second oldest in the nation. Because it's on active duty, the public is not able to tour the inside, but a boardwalk nearby gives nice views.

British Cemetery

The British Cemetery (British Cemetery Rd.) is not, as one might suppose, a colonial burial, but rather a vestige of World War II. During the war, the Carolina coast was lousy with German U-boats. Many old-timers today remember catching a glimpse of a furtive German sub casing the beach. Defending the Outer Banks became a pressing concern, and on May 11, 1942, the HMS *Bedfordshire,* a British trawler sent to aid the U.S. Navy, was torpedoed by a German U-558. The *Bedfordshire* sank, and all 37 men aboard died. Over the course of the next week, four bodies washed up on Ocracoke—those of Lieutenant Thomas Cunningham, Ordinary Telegraphist Stanley Craig, and two unidentified men. An island family donated a burial plot, and there the four men lie today, memorialized with a plaque that bears a lovely verse by Rupert Brooke, the young poet of World War I and member of the British Navy, who died of disease on his way to the battle of Gallipoli.

Sports and Recreation

Ride the Wind Surf Shop gives individual and group surfing lessons, for adults and children, covering ocean safety and surfing etiquette in addition to board handling. A three-day surf camp for kids ages 9–17 ($200, or $75/day) gives an even more in-depth tutorial. Ride the Wind also leads sunrise, sunset, and full-moon kayak tours around the marshes of Ocracoke ($35).

The **Schooner Windfall** (departs from Community Store Dock, Ocracoke, 252/928-7245, www.schoonerwindfall.com), a beautiful 57-foot, old-fashioned-looking schooner, sails on three one-hour tours a day around Pamlico Sound. Passengers are allowed, and even encouraged, to try their hand at the wheel or trimming the sails.

Accommodations

The **Captain's Landing** (324 Hwy. 12, 252/928-1999, www.thecaptainslanding.com, from $200 in-season, from $100 out of season), with a perch right on Silver Lake (the harbor) looking towards the lighthouse, is a modern hotel owned by a descendant of Ocracoke's oldest families. Suites have 1.5 baths, full kitchens, comfortable sleeper sofas for extra guests, and decks with beautiful views. They also have a bright, airy penthouse with two bedrooms, an office, a gourmet kitchen, and even a laundry room. The Captain's Cottage is a private two-bedroom house, also smack on the water, with great decks and its own courtyard.

The **Pony Island Motel and Cottages** (785 Irvin Garrish Hwy., 866/928-4411, www.pony islandmotel.com, from $108 in-season, from $60 out of season) has been in operation since the late 1950s, and run by the same family for more than 40 years. It has regular and efficiency motel rooms, and four cottages on the grounds. Clean rooms, a good location, and year-round good prices make this a top choice on the island.

Edwards of Ocracoke (800/254-1359, www.edwardsofocracoke.com, from $53 spring and fall, from $90 summer) has several cozy bungalows typical of coastal Carolina, referred to here as "vintage accommodations." The mid-20th century vacation ambiance is very pleasant, the cabins are clean and well kept, and prices are great.

The **Island Inn** (25 Lighthouse Rd., 252/928-

4351, www.ocracokeislandinn.com, from $60 out of season, from $100 in-season, no children) is on the National Register of Historic Places, and bills itself as the oldest operating business on the Outer Banks. It was built in 1901, first used as an Odd Fellows Hall, later as a barracks during World War II. The building is made of salvaged shipwreck wood, which everyone knows brings strange juju; add that fact to the 1950s murder of a caretaker, and the discovery of colonial bones under the lobby, and it's a given that the place is haunted. The resident wraith is believed to be a lady ghost, because she seems to enjoy checking out female guests' cosmetics and clothes, which will sometimes turn up in the morning in places other than where they were left the night before. No one's ever seen her, but her footsteps are sometimes heard in empty rooms, and she causes odd things to happen—most notably, unraveling an entire roll of toilet paper in the presence of a terrified guest. Like many hotel ghosts, she is most active during the inn's less crowded seasons.

CAMPING

At **Ocracoke Campground** (4352 Irvin Garrish Hwy., Ocracoke, 877/444-6777, $23/night), campsites are right by the beach, behind the dunes. Remember to bring extra-long stakes to anchor your tent in the sand.

Food

Ocracoke's **Café Atlantic** (1129 Irvin Garris Hwy., 252/928-4861, www.ocracokeisland .com/cafe_atlantic.htm, $14–21) has a large and eclectic menu, with tastes venturing into Italian, Nuevo Latino, and local fare. Lunch and dinner choices can be as simple as a BLT or a crab cake (with Pamlico Sound crabmeat), to *caciucco,* an Italian seafood stew. While many restaurants will accommodate vegetarians with a single pasta dish at the end of the entrée list, Café Atlantic has tons of non-meat-or-seafood options. They've also got an extensive wine list.

GETTING THERE AND AROUND

The northern part of Cape Hatteras National Seashore can be reached by car, by following Route 12 south from Nags Head. Following 12 you'll go through the towns of Rodanthe, Waves, Salvo, and Avon, then around the tip of the cape to Buxton, Frisco, and Hatteras, where the highway ends. From there, you have two choices: backtrack, or hop a ferry.

Ocracoke can only be reached by ferry. The Hatteras-Ocracoke Ferry (800/368-8949, free, 40 min.) is the shortest route to Ocracoke. If you look at a map, Highway 12 is shown crossing from Ocracoke to Cedar Island, as if there's an impossibly long bridge over Pamlico Sound. In fact, that stretch of Highway 12 is a ferry route too. The **Cedar Island-Ocracoke Ferry** (800/856-0343, www.ncdot.org/transit/ferry), which is a 2.25-hour ride, costs $15 per regular-sized vehicle, one-way. There's also a ferry between Ocracoke and Swan Quarter (800/345-1665, $15/regular-sized vehicle, one-way, 2.5 hours).

Across the Sounds

Referred to historically as the Albemarle, and sometimes today as the Inner Banks, the mainland portion of northeastern North Carolina is the hearth of the state's colonial history, the site of its first European towns and earliest plantation and maritime economies.

The Great Dismal Swamp is here, a region thought of by early Carolinians and Virginians as a diseased and haunted wasteland, the sooner drained the better. They succeeded to some extent in beating back the swamp waters and vapors, but left enough for modern generations to recognize as one of the state's crown jewels, a natural feature as valuable to humans as to the bears and wolves who hide within.

Early cities like Edenton and Bath were influential centers of government and commerce, and today preserve some of the best colonial and early federal architecture in the Southeast. The vast network of rivers and creeks include some of the state's best canoeing and kayaking waters, and along the Albemarle Regional Canoe/Kayak Trail, there are a growing number of camping platforms on which to spend an unforgettable night listening to owls hoot and otters splash. Country kitchens are found throughout the small towns here, and there are even a few old-fashioned fish shacks in which to sample the inland seafood traditions. Water is the soul of this region, with the Sounds and the rivers and swamps guiding life on the land as surely as if it were touched by the ocean.

◖ THE GREAT DISMAL SWAMP

Viewed for centuries as an impediment to progress, the Great Dismal Swamp is now recognized for the national treasure that it is, and tens of thousands of acres are protected. There are several points from which to gain access to the interior of the Dismal Swamp. A few miles south of the Carolina/Virginia line, on U.S. 17, is the **Dismal Swamp Welcome Center** (2294 Hwy. 17 N., visitors center at 2356 Hwy. 17 N., South Mills, 877/771-8333, www.dismalswamp.com, 9 A.M.–5 P.M. daily Memorial Day–Halloween, 9 A.M.–5 P.M. Tues.–Sat. the rest of the year). Should you be arriving by water, you'll find the Welcome Center at Mile 28 on the Intracoastal Waterway. You can tie up to the dock here and spend the night, if you wish, or wait for one of the four daily lock openings (8:30 A.M., 11 A.M., 1:30 P.M., and 3:30 P.M.) to proceed. There are also picnic tables and grills here, and restrooms open day and night.

Another area of the swamp to explore is the **Great Dismal Swamp National Wildlife Refuge** (Suffolk, VA, 757/986-3705, www.albemarle-nc.com/gates/gdsnwr, open daylight hours), which straddles the state line. Two main entrances are outside of Suffolk, Virginia, off the White Marsh Road/Route 642. These entrances, Washington Ditch and Jericho Lane, are open 6:30 A.M.–8 P.M. daily between April 1–September 30, and 6:30 A.M.–5 P.M. October 1–March 31. In the middle of the refuge is Lake Drummond, an eerie 3,100-acre natural lake that's a wonderful place for canoeing. (Contact refuge headquarters for directions on navigating the feeder ditch that lets out into Lake Drummond.) You may see all sorts of wildlife in the swamp—including poisonous cottonmouths, canebrake rattlers, and copperheads, and possibly even black bears. One more word of caution: Controlled hunting is permitted on certain days in October, November, and December, so if visiting in the fall, wear bright clothing, and contact refuge staff in advance of your visit to find out about closures.

GATESVILLE

Near the town of Gatesville, a little ways west of South Mills on Highway 158, is another gorgeous swampy natural area, **Merchant's Millpond State Park** (176 Millpond Rd., Gatesville, 252/357-1191, www.ncparks.gov/Visit/parks/memi/main.php, office open 8 A.M.–4:30 P.M. daily except state holidays, park open 8 A.M.–6 P.M. November–February, 8 A.M.–8 P.M. March–May, 8 A.M.–9 P.M. June–August, 8 A.M.–8 P.M. September and October). The variety of wildlife here is quite amazing, particularly among the reptile delegation—many kinds of snakes (most harmless) and turtles (harmless, except for the snappers), and, despite the relatively northerly clime, alligators (most emphatically not harmless). There are all manner of other creatures too, from salamanders to mink and nutria.

This is a great spot for canoeing or kayaking, with miles of beautiful blackwater backwaters. The park has a canoe rental facility, charging $5/hour for the first hour and $3/hour for each additional hour; or, for those camping, $20 for a 24-hour period. There are several hiking trails through the park, totaling about nine miles. Park officials classify all the trails as easy, but strongly caution that hikers need to be careful to avoid ticks. They recommend that you wear bug spray, tuck pants legs into socks, and wear light-colored clothes so as to be able to see ticks better.

Merchant's Millpond has several campsites, for three kinds of campers. The family campground, near the park office, is easily accessible, accommodates trailers as well as tents, and had a washhouse with restrooms, showers, and drinking water. Off the park's Lassiter trail are five backpack campsites. All supplies, including water, must be packed in, and there is a pit toilet nearby. There are also two canoe camping areas reached by canoe trails. These sites too have pit toilets, and campers must bring water and other supplies.

ELIZABETH CITY

The **Museum of the Albemarle** (501 S. Water St., 252/335-1453, www.museumofthe albemarle.com, 9 A.M.–5 P.M. Tues.–Sat., 2–5 P.M. Sun.) is a relatively new, and growing, museum. It explores the four centuries of history in northeastern North Carolina since the first English settlers arrived at Roanoke. Come here to learn about the Lost Colonists, the pirates who swarmed in this region, the folkways of the Sound country, and more.

To stay in Elizabeth City, you have several options. The **Pond House Inn** (915 Rivershore Rd., 252/335-9834, www.thepondhouseinn .com, $99–165) sits on the banks of the Pasquotank. Each of the large guestrooms has its own fireplace in this pleasant 1940s house. The **Culpepper Inn** (609 W. Main St., 252/335-9235, www.culpepperinn.com, $90–145), just a few blocks from the Albemarle Sound, has several comfortable guest rooms in the main house, and cozy accommodations in a carriage house and cottage.

There are also chain motels in the area, ranging from the **Travelers Inn** (1211 N. Road St., 252/338-5451, www.travelersinn .webs.com, around $70, small pets allowed) and **Econo Lodge** (522 S. Hughes Blvd. B, 252/338-4124, www.econolodge.com, around $70, pets allowed) to the **Holiday Inn Express** (306 S. Hughes Blvd., 252/338-8900, www .hiexpress.com, $75–125) and **Hampton Inn** (402 Halstead Blvd., 252/333-1800, www .hamptoninn.com, around $100).

HERTFORD

If you're traveling between Edenton and Elizabeth City, don't miss Hertford, a pretty little Spanish moss-draped town on the Perquimans (per-KWIH-muns) River. The historic **Newbold White House** (151 Newbold White Rd., 252/426-7567, www.newbold whitehouse.org, guided tours 10 A.M.–4 P.M. Tuesday–Saturday March 1–Thanksgiving, $5 adults, $3 students) is the oldest brick house in North Carolina, built in 1730 by one of the region's early Quakers. The grounds include a seasonal herb garden and a 17th-century Quaker graveyard. While you're in Hertford, stop in at **Woodard's Pharmacy** (101 N. Church St., 252/426-5527) an old-fashioned lunch counter and soda fountain in the heart of downtown, where you can grab a pimiento cheese sandwich and an ice cream cone. If you're making it an overnight, stay at **1812 on the Perquimans** (385 Old Neck Rd., 252/426-1812, $80–85), or at the **Beechtree Inn** (948 Pender Rd., 252/426-1593, $90). At the Beechtree, guests stay in restored pre-Civil War cottages. Children and pets are welcome.

EDENTON

Incorporated in 1722 but inhabited long before that, Edenton was one of North Carolina's most important colonial towns, and remains one of its most beautiful.

Historic District

The whole town is lined with historic buildings, and several especially important sites are clustered within a few blocks of each other near the waterfront. The easiest starting point for a walking tour (guided or on your own) is the headquarters of the **Edenton State Historic Site** (108 N. Broad St., 252/482-2637, www.edenton.nchistoricsites .org, 9 A.M.–5 P.M. Mon.–Sat. and 1–5 P.M. Sun. Apr.–Oct., 10 A.M.–4 P.M. Mon.–Sat. and 1–4 P.M. Sun. Nov.–Mar.), also referred to as the Edenton Visitors Center. The 1782 **Barker House** (505 S. Broad St., 252/482-7800, www.edentonhistoricalcommission.org,

10 A.M.–4 P.M. Mon.–Sat., 1–4 P.M. Sun.), a stunning Lowcountry palazzo, was the home of Penelope Barker, an early revolutionary and organizer of the Edenton Tea Party. It's now the headquarters of the Edenton Historical Commission, and the location of their bookstore. The 1758 **Cupola House** (108 Broad St., 252/482-2637, www.cupolahouse.org, 9 A.M.–4:30 P.M. daily, tickets available at Edenton Visitors Center) is a National Historical Landmark, a home of great architectural significance. Although much of the original interior woodwork was removed in 1918 and sold to the Brooklyn Museum, where it remains, the Cupola House has been restored meticulously inside and out, and its colonial gardens re-created. Also a designated National Historical Landmark is the **Chowan County Courthouse** (111 E. King St., 252/482-2637, www.edenton.nchistoricsites.org, hours vary by season), a superb 1767 brick building in the Georgian style. It's the best-preserved colonial courthouse in the United States.

Accommodations and Food

The Ⓒ **Broad Street Inn** (300 N. Broad St., 888/394-6622, www.edentoninn.com, from $170) occupies not one but four exceptional historic buildings: the 1901 main White-Bond House, the 1801 Satterfield House, a 1915 tobacco storage barn remodeled with beautiful guestrooms, and the 1870 Tillie Bond House cottage. Each one of these is artfully restored, with soft and restful furnishings. Breakfast cook Janie Granby prepares specialties like lemon soufflé pancakes, and North Carolina native and star chef Kevin Yokley prepares four-course dinners that are dazzling. Entrées include grilled swordfish with artichoke vinaigrette, lamb porterhouse chops with dried cherry sauce, and breast of Muscovy duck with red currant sauce.

The **Granville Queen Inn** (108 S. Granville St., 866/482-8534, www.granvillequeen.com, $95–140) is a rather splendid early-1900s mansion decorated in a variety of early 20th-century styles. Breakfasts are as ornate and elegant as the house itself, featuring poached pears, potato tortillas, crepes, and much more.

WINDSOR

A small, historic town on the Cashie River, Windsor is the county seat of Bertie County. Historic architecture, good food, and wetlands exploration are equally compelling reasons to visit this lesser-known treasure of the Albemarle region. Pronunciation is a little perverse here: The county name is pronounced "Ber-TEE," and the river is the "Cuh-SHY."

Sights

Hope Plantation (132 Hope House Rd., 252/794-3140, www.hopeplantation.org, 10 A.M.–5 P.M. Mon.–Sat. and 2–5 P.M. Sun. Apr.–Oct., 10 A.M.–4 P.M. Mon.–Sat. and 2–5 P.M. Sun. Nov.–Mar., $8, $7 seniors, $3 under 18) was built in 1803 for the former Governor David Stone. Stone did not live to see his 50th birthday, but by the time of his death he had been the governor of North Carolina, a U.S. senator and congressman, a state senator, a Superior Court judge, and a seven-times-elected member of the State House. He graduated from Princeton and passed the bar when he was 20; he was the father of 11 children, and one of the founders of the University of North Carolina. High among his most impressive accomplishments was the construction of this wonderful house. Characterized by a mixture of Georgian and Federal styles with significant twists of regional and individual aesthetics, Hope House is on the National Register of Historic Places. Also on the National Register, and now on the grounds of the plantation, is the brick-end, gambrel roof King-Bazemore House. The King-Bazemore House was built in 1763, and is also a highly significant example of its form.

The **Roanoke-Cashie River Center** (112 W. Water St., Windsor, 252/794-2001, www.partnershipforthesounds.org/Roanoke CashieRiverCenter.aspx, 10 A.M.–4 P.M. Tues.–Sat., $2, $1 children) has interpretive exhibits about this region's history and ecology. There

© ELAINE FORMAN

Hope Plantation, near Windsor

is a canoe ramp outside where you can get out into the Cashie River, and canoe rentals are available ($10/hour, $25 for a half-day, and $35 for a whole day).

Southeast of Windsor on the Cashie River, the **San Souci Ferry** (Woodard and San Souci Rds., 252/794-4277, 6:30 A.M.–6 P.M. Mar. 16–Sept. 16, 6:45 A.M.–5 P.M. Sept. 17–March 15) operates, as it has for generations, by a cable and a honk of the horn. To cross the river, pull up to the bank, honk your horn, and wait. Directly the ferryman will emerge and pull you across.

Recreation
The headquarters of the **Roanoke River National Wildlife Refuge** (114 W. Water St., 252/794-3808, www.fws.gov/roanokeriver) are located here in Windsor. The Refuge, however, stretches over nearly 21,000 acres in Bertie County, through the hardwood bottomlands and cypress-tupelo wetlands of the Roanoke

River Valleys, an environment that the Nature Conservancy calls "one of the last great places." The Refuge is an exceptional place for bird-watching, with the largest inland heron rookery in North Carolina, a large population of bald eagles, and many wintering waterfowl and neo-tropical migrant species.

Food
Bunn's Bar-B-Q (127 N. King St., 252/794-2274, from $5) is a barbeque and Brunswick stew joint of renown, an early gas station converted in 1938 to its present state. Super-finely chopped barbeque is the specialty, with cole-slaw, cornbread, and plenty of sauce from those little red bottles you see on every surface.

SCOTLAND NECK
In the little Halifax County community of Scotland Neck, west of Windsor, is the **Sylvan Heights Waterfowl Center and Eco-Park** (4963 Hwy. 258, 252/826-3186,

www.shwpark.com, 9 A.M.–5 P.M. Apr. 1–Sept. 30, 9 A.M.–4 P.M. Oct. 1–March 31, closed Mondays, open Memorial Day and Labor Day, adults $7, children up to age 12 $5, seniors over 62 $5, children under 2 free). This center for the conservation of rare species of birds is home to the world's largest collection of waterfowl, comprised of more than 1,000 birds and 170 different species. A visit to Sylvan Heights is an unbeatable occasion to get up very close to birds you might never have another chance to encounter. It's also a great opportunity for wildlife photography—you won't even need your zoom lens.

WILLIAMSTON AND VICINITY

Williamston is at the junction of U.S. 17 and U.S. 64. If you're passing through town, Williamston is a great place to stop for barbecue or a fresh seafood meal.

Sights

A little west of Williamston on U.S. 13/64 Alt., you'll find the town of Robersonville and

ROANOKE RIVER

After a long journey down from the Blue Ridge Mountains of Virginia, the waters of the Roanoke River cross into North Carolina just northwest of the town of Roanoke Rapids, and travel another 130 miles before emptying into the Albemarle Sound. The Roanoke River has played a crucial role in the region's history, a major route for transportation and commerce in colonial times. It is also a river of tremendous ecological importance. The river's floodplain represents the Mid-Atlantic's largest and most pristine bottomland hardwood forest ecosystem. It's a region of beautifully primitive, dark swamps and towering ancient trees.

More than 100,000 acres surrounding the river are preserved as wild places. The **Roanoke River National Wildlife Refuge** (headquarters: 114 Water St., Windsor, 252/794 3808, http://roanokeriver.fws.gov) encompasses more than 20,000 acres in three separate tracts – Broadneck Swamp, Company Swamp, and Conine Island – between the towns of Hamilton and Windsor. Limited road access is available from Highway 17 north of Windsor, but the best way to experience the refuge is by water. The Nature Conservancy also owns tens of thousands of acres of forests and wetlands along the river. These areas can be explored on field trips led by the North Carolina chapter of the **Nature Conservancy** (www.nature.org/wherewework/northamerica/states/northcarolina).

For a lover of river journeys by canoe or kayak, this is an irresistible place, and thanks to a network of area environmental and community organizations, it is increasingly a destination for paddlers. **Roanoke River Partners** (252/792-0070 or 252/724-0352, www.roanokeriverpartners.org) has designated a paddle trail through this wild region. They've also constructed more than a dozen camping platforms at locations along the river, from Weldon, near the Virginia line, to Albemarle Sound. Every camping platform is different, but most are sturdy wooden decks over the cypress swamps or in the woods near the river, on which campers can pitch their tents. Others are positively cushy screen houses in which campers can sleep protected from hovering bugs.

Reservations are required in order to use the platforms, and there's a lot to learn before you embark on a Roanoke River trip. (For instance, do you know what to do if a bear pays a visit to your campsite? At some of the campsites, that information may come in handy.) Read the information on the Roanoke River Partners website, or give them a call to find out more. Some stretches of the trail are best suited to experienced paddlers and campers. Novices can enjoy the river too, though, by signing up for guided trips with conservation organizations (such as the Nature Conservancy), paddle clubs, like the **Roanoke Paddle Club** (www.roanokepaddleclub.webs.com), or commercial river guides. Durham-based **Frog Hollow Outfitters** (919/949-4315, www.froghollowoutfitters.com), for example, leads trips on many North Carolina rivers, including the Roanoke.

the **St. James Place Museum** (U.S. 64 Alt. and Outerbridge Rd., open year-round by appointment, call Robersonville Public Library at 252/795-3591). A Primitive Baptist church built in 1910 and restored by a local preservationist and folk art enthusiast, St. James Place is an unusual little museum that fans of Southern craft will not want to miss. A serious collection of traditional quilts is the main feature of the museum. Of the 100 on display, nearly half are African American quilts—examples of which are much less likely to survive and find their way into museum collections than are their counterpane counterparts made by white quilters. Getting a glimpse of the two traditions side by side is an education in these parallel Southern aesthetics.

On the same highway is **East Carolina Motor Speedway** (4918 U.S. 64 Alt., 252/795-3968, www.ecmsracing.com, pits open at 3 P.M., grandstands at 5 P.M., usually Apr.–Oct.), a 0.4-mile hard-surface track featuring several divisions, including late-model street stock, modified street-stock, super stock four-cylinder, and four-cylinder kids' class.

Food

Come to Williamston on an empty stomach. It has an assortment of old and very traditional eateries. The **C Sunny Side Oyster Bar** (1102 Washington St., 252/792-3416, www.sunnysideoysterbarnc.com, open from 5:30 P.M. Mon.–Sat. and from 5 P.M. Sun., Sept.–Apr., www.sunnysideoysterbarnc.com) is the best known, a seasonal oyster joint open in the months with the letter R—that is, oyster season. It's been in business since 1935, and is a historic as well as gastronomic landmark. Oysters are steamed behind the restaurant, and then hauled inside and shucked at the bar. Visit the restaurant's website to acquaint yourselves with the shuckers. In eastern North Carolina, a good oyster shucker is regarded as highly as a good artist or athlete, and rightly so. The Sunny Side doesn't take reservations, and it fills to capacity in no time flat, so come early.

Down the road a piece, **Martin Supply** (118 Washington St., 252/792-2123), an old general

store, is a good place to buy local produce and preserves, honey, molasses, and hoop cheese. **Griffin's Quick Lunch** (204 Washington St., 252/792-0002) is a popular old diner with good barbecue. Back on U.S. 64, **Shaw's Barbecue** (U.S. 64 Alt., 252/792-5339) serves eastern Carolina-style barbecue, as well as good greasy breakfasts.

East of Williamston at the intersection of U.S. 64 and Highway 171, the small Roanoke River town of Jamesville is home to a most unusual restaurant that draws attention from all over the country (it's even been featured in the *New York Times*). The **C Cypress Grill** (1520 Stewart St. off U.S. 64, 252/792-4175) is an unprepossessing wooden shack right-smack on the river, a survivor of the days when Jamesville made its living in the herring industry, dragging the fish out of the water with horse-drawn seine nets. Herring—breaded and seriously deep-fried, not pickled or sweet—is the main dish here, though they also dress the herring up in other outfits, and serve bass, flounder, perch, oyster, catfish, and other fish too. The Cypress Grill is open for the three and a half months of the year (from the second Thurs. in Jan. through the end of Apr.), and you could hardly have a more intensely authentic, small-town dining experience anywhere else.

EAST ON U.S. 64

The eastern stretch of U.S. 64 runs along the Albemarle Sound between Williamston and the Outer Banks, passing through the towns of Plymouth, Creswell, and Columbia before it crosses over to Roanoke Island. Here you'll encounter evidence of North Carolina's ancient past, old-growth forests; recent past, a plantation with a long and complex history of slavery; and the present, art galleries and abundant wildlife-watching and recreational opportunities.

Plymouth

Plymouth is an attractive little town on the Roanoke River, with a rich maritime and military history. Most notably, it was the site of the 1864 Battle of Plymouth, the second-largest Civil War battle in North Carolina, fought by more than 20,000 men. At the **Roanoke River Lighthouse and Maritime Museum** (W. Water St., 252/217-2204, www.roanoke riverlighthouse.org, 11 A.M.–3 P.M. Tues.–Sat., and by appointment), visitors can explore a pretty replica of Plymouth's 1866 screwpile lighthouse and, across the street in an old car dealership, the maritime museum itself, featuring artifacts and photographs from the region's waterfaring heritage. On East Water Street is the **Port O'Plymouth Museum** (302 E. Water St., 252/793-1377, www.livinghistoryweekend .com/port_o.htm). This tiny museum is packed with Civil War artifacts, including a collection of beautiful pistols, telling the story of the Battle of Plymouth.

Davenport Homestead

West of Creswell is the Davenport Homestead (about three miles from Exit 554 off U.S. 64, 252/793-1377), a small 18th-century cabin built by Daniel Davenport, the first state senator from Washington County. In 1800 this diminutive homestead was home to 14 people—six members of the Davenport family, and eight slaves. Visitors can take a self-guided tour of the Davenport Homestead, but for a closer look, ask Loretta Phelps, who lives across the road and is a Davenport descendant, to unlock the buildings and show you around.

◖ Somerset Place Historic Site

Somerset Place Historic Site (2572 Lake Shore Rd., Creswell, 252/797-4560, www.ah.dcr .state.nc.us/Sections/hs/somerset/somerset. htm, 9 A.M.–5 P.M. Mon.–Sat. and 1–5 P.M. Sun. Apr.–Oct., 10 A.M.–4 P.M. Tues.–Sat and 1–4 P.M. Sun. Nov.–Mar., free) was one of North Carolina's largest and most profitable plantations for the 80 years leading up to the Civil War. In the late 18th century and early 19th centuries, 80 Africa-born men, women, and children were brought to Somerset to labor in the fields. The grief and spiritual disorientation they experienced, and the subsequent trials of the slave community that grew to include more than 300 people, are told by the historian Dorothy Spruill Redford in the amazing book *Somerset*

© SARAH BRYAN

The plantation house at Somerset Place sits on the banks of Lake Phelps.

Homecoming. Somerset is a significant place from many historical standpoints, but the story of its African American community makes it one of this state's most important historic sites.

Somerset Place is an eerily lovely place to visit. The restored grounds and buildings, including the Collins family's house, slave quarters, and several dependencies, are deafeningly quiet, and the huge cypress trees growing right up to the quarters and the mansion make the place feel almost prehistoric. Visitors are permitted to walk around the estate at their leisure. A small bookshop on the grounds is a good source for books about North Carolina history in general, and African American history in particular.

Pettigrew State Park

On the banks of **Lake Phelps,** Pettigrew State Park (2252 Lakeshore Rd., Creswell, 252/797-4475, www.ncparks.gov/Visit/parks/pett/main.php) preserves a weird ancient waterscape that's unlike anywhere else in the state. Archaeology reveals that there was a human presence here a staggering 10,000 years ago. The lake, which

© BILL SWINDAMAN

Cypress trees line the banks of Lake Phelps.

is five miles across, has yielded more than 30 ancient dugout canoes, some as much as 4,000 years old and measuring more than 30 feet. The natural surroundings are ancient too, encompassing some of eastern North Carolina's only remaining old-growth forests. **Pungo Lake,** a smaller body of water within the park, is visited by 50,000 migrating snow geese over the course of the year, an unforgettable sight for wildlife watchers.

Visitors to Pettigrew State Park can camp at the family campground ($15/day), which has drive-to sites and access to restrooms and hot showers, or at primitive group campsites (starting at $9/day).

Art Galleries

Pocosin Arts (corner of Main and Water Sts., Columbia, 252/796-2787, www.pocosinarts.org, 10 A.M.–5 P.M. Tues.–Sat.) has helped spur a renaissance of craft in Eastern North Carolina, teaching community classes in ceramics, fiber arts, sculpture, jewelry making, metalwork, and many other arts. At the sales gallery, beautiful handmade items are available for purchase, and the main gallery displays many kinds of folk art from Eastern North Carolina.

Sports and Recreation

Palmetto-Peartree Preserve (entrance is east of Columbia on Pot Licker Rd./Loop Rd./SR 1220, 252/796-0723 or 919/967-2223, www.palmettopeartree.org) is a 10,000-acre natural area, wrapped in 14 miles of shoreline along the Albemarle Sound and Little Alligator Creek. Originally established as a sanctuary for the red cockaded woodpecker, this is a great location for bird-watching and spotting other wildlife (which include, in addition to the birds, alligators, wolves, bears, and bobcats); hiking, biking, and horseback riding along the old logging trails through the forest; and canoeing and kayaking. The preserve's excellent paddle trail passes by Hidden Lake, a secluded cypress-swamp blackwater lake. There is an overnight camping platform at the lake, which can be used in the daytime without a permit for bird-watching and picnicking. To stay overnight, arrange for a permit through the Roanoke River Partners (252/792-3790, www.roanokeriverpartners.org).

Once the southern edge of the Great Dismal Swamp, **Pocosin Lakes National Wildlife Refuge** (headquarters at Walter B. Jones, Sr., Center for the Sounds, U.S. 64, six miles south of Columbia, 252/796-3004, www.fws.gov/pocosinlakes) is an important haven for many species of animals, including migratory waterfowl, and re-introduced red wolves. Five important bodies of water lie within the refuge: Pungo Lake, New Lake, the 16,600-acre Lake Phelps, and stretches of the Scuppernong and Alligator Rivers. All of these areas are good spots for observing migratory waterfowl, but Pungo Lake is particularly special in the fall and winter, when snow geese and tundra swans visit in massive numbers—approaching 100,000—on their round-trip Arctic journeys.

The landscape here was drastically altered by a tremendous wildfire that burned for days in the summer of 2008, blanketing towns as far away as Raleigh with thick smoke. Wildfire is an important part of the natural cycle here, however, and now is a unique opportunity to watch the regeneration of an ecosystem.

Also east of Columbia on U.S. 64 is the **Alligator River National Wildlife Refuge** (between Columbia and Roanoke Island, 252/473-1131, http://alligatorriver.fws.gov). The large refuge covers most of the peninsula that lies between the Alligator River to the west, Albemarle Sound to the north, Croatan Sound to the east, and Pamlico Sound to the southeast. This large swath of woods and pocosin represents one of the most important wildlife habitats in the state, home to over 200 species of birds, as well as alligators, red wolves, and more black bears than almost anywhere in the coastal Mid-Atlantic. In the 1980s red wolves were introduced into the Alligator River Refuge as they became extinct in the wild elsewhere in their original range. During the summer months, the Columbia-based **Red Wolf Coalition** (252.796.5600, http://redwolves.com) leads "howlings," nighttime

expeditions into the refuge to hear the wolves' calling through the woods. Reservations are required, and participation usually costs $7, though is free on certain occasions. Visit the Red Wolf Coalition's website for details. There are many other ways to enjoy the Alligator River National Wildlife Refuge, most popular among them hiking, kayaking, and bird-watching. Though at this writing the refuge does not have a physical headquarters, there are plans to build one in Manteo in the coming years. In the meantime, detailed directions and visitor information can be found on the refuge website.

WASHINGTON, BATH, AND BELHAVEN
On the north side of the Pamlico River, as you head towards Mattamuskeet National Wildlife Refuge and the Outer Banks, the towns of Washington, Bath, and Belhaven offer short diversions into the nature and history of this region.

North Carolina Estuarium
The North Carolina Estuarium (223 E. Water St., Washington, 252/948-0000, www.partnershipforthesounds.org/NorthCarolinaEstuarium.aspx, 10 A.M.–4 P.M. Tues.–Sat., $3, $2 children) is a museum about both the natural and cultural history of the Tar-Pamlico River basin. In addition to the exhibits, which include live native animals, historic artifacts, and much more, the Estuarium operates pontoon boat tours on the Pamlico River. River roving is free, but reservations are required.

Turnage Theater
Washington has a great performing arts facility in the restored early 20th-century Turnage Theater (150 W. Main St., Washington, 252/975-1711, www.turnagetheater.com). All sorts of performances take place at the Turnage throughout the year, including prominent artists from around the country. There are concerts of all kinds of music, productions by touring dance troupes and regional theater companies, and screenings of classic movies.

THE OUTER BANKS

Moss House

Located in the historic district, a block from the river, is the Moss House (129 Van Norden St., 252/975-3967, www.themosshouse.com, $110–235). This 1902 house is a cozy bed-and-breakfast with airy rooms and delicious breakfasts. An easy walk from the Moss House is **Bill's Hot Dogs** (109 Gladden St., 252/946-3343), a longtime local favorite for a quick snack.

Goose Creek State Park

Goose Creek State Park (2190 Camp Leach Rd., 252/923-2191, www.ncparks.gov/Visit/parks/gocr/main.php) lies on the banks of the Pamlico, where Goose Creek empties into the river. It's an exotic environment of brackish marshes, freshwater swamps, and tall pine forests, home to a variety of wildlife, including bears, a multitude of bird species, and rather many snakes. More than eight miles of hiking trails, as well as boardwalks and paddle tails, traverse the hardwood swamp environment. Twelve primitive campsites, with access to toilets and water, are available year-round, including one that is handicapped-accessible.

Historic Bath

North Carolina's oldest town, Bath was chartered in 1705. The town is so little changed that even today it is mostly contained within the original boundaries laid out by the explorer John Lawson. For its first 70 or so years, Bath enjoyed the spotlight as one of North Carolina's most important centers of trade and politics—home of governors, refuge from Indian wars, frequent host to and victim of Blackbeard. Much as Brunswick Town, to the south, was made redundant by the growth of Wilmington, Bath faded into obscurity as the town of Washington grew in the years after the Revolution. Today almost all of Bath is designated as Historic Bath (252/923-3971, www.bath.nchistoricsites.org, visitors center and tours 9 A.M.–5 P.M. Mon.–Sat. and 1–5 P.M. Sun. Apr.–Oct., 10 A.M.–4 P.M. Tues.–Sat. and 1–4 P.M. Sun. Nov.–Mar., admission charged for the Palmer-Marsh and Bonner Houses). Important sites on the tour of the village are

the 1734 St. Thomas Church, 1751 Palmer-Marsh House, 1790 Van Der Veer House, 1830 Bonner House, and, from time immemorial, a set of indelible hoofprints said to have been made by the devil's own horse.

While in Bath, drop in at the **Old Town Country Kitchen** (436 Carteret St., 252/923-1840) for some country cooking and seafood. If you decide to stay the night, try the **Inn on Bath Creek** (116 S. Main St., 252/923-9571, www.innonbathcreek.com, $130–225, two-night reservation required for Friday or Saturday nights between April and November). This bed-and-breakfast, built on the site of the former Buzzard Hotel, fits in nicely with the old architecture of the historic town, but because it was built in 1999, has modern conveniences to make your stay especially comfortable.

Belhaven

The name of **Belhaven Memorial Museum** (210 E. Main St., Belhaven, 252/943-6817, www.beaufort-county.com/Belhaven/museum/Belhaven.htm, 1–5 P.M. Thurs.–Tues.) gives no hint as to what a very strange little institution this is. The museum houses the collection of Miss Eva—Eva Blount Way, who died in 1962 at the age of 92—surely one of the most accomplished collectors of oddities ever. The local paper wrote of her in 1951 that, "housewife, snake killer, curator, trapper, dramatic actress, philosopher, and preserver of all the riches of mankind, inadequately describes the most fascinating person you can imagine." Miss Eva kept among her earthly treasures a collection of pickled tumors (one weighs 10 pounds), a pickled one-eyed pig, a pickled two-headed kitten, cataracts (pickled), and three pickled human babies. There's also a dress that belonged to a 700-pound woman, a flea couple dressed in wedding togs, 30,000 buttons, and assorted snakes that Miss Eva determined needed killing. It must have taken a very long time to carry everything over here, but Miss Eva's collection is now on public display, the core of the Belhaven Memorial Museum's collection.

Belhaven has an especially nice inn, the **Belhaven Water Street Bed and Breakfast**

(567 E. Water St., 866/338-2825, www.belhaven waterstreetbandb.com, $85–115). The guest rooms in this hundred-year-old house face Pantego Creek, and have their own fireplaces and private bathrooms, as well as wireless access.

◖ MATTAMUSKEET NATIONAL WILDLIFE REFUGE

Near the tiny town of Swan Quarter, the Mattamuskeet National Wildlife Refuge (Hwy. 94, between Swan Quarter and Englehard, 252/926-4021, www.fws.gov/mattamuskeet) preserves one of North Carolina's most remarkable natural features, as well as one of its most famous buildings. Lake Mattamuskeet, 18 miles long by 6 miles wide, is the state's largest natural lake, and being an average of a foot and half deep—five feet at its deepest point—it is a most unusual environment. The hundreds of thousands of waterfowl who rest here on their seasonal rounds make this a world-famous location for bird-watching and wildlife photography.

Old-timers in the area have fond memories of dancing at the **Lodge at Lake Mattamuskeet,** one of eastern North Carolina's best-known buildings. The huge old building was constructed in 1915, and was at the time the world's largest pumping station, moving over one million gallons of water per minute. In 1934, it was bought by the federal government along with the wildlife sanctuary, and the Civilian Conservation Corps transformed it into the lodge that was a favorite gathering place for the next 40 years. The lodge is closed at the time of this writing, but is undergoing restoration for future public use.

Hiking and biking trails thread through the refuge, but camping is not permitted. In season, beware of hunters and keep an eye out as well for copperheads, cottonmouths, two kinds of rattlesnakes, and alligators. Bears and red wolves abound as well. Within the administration of the Mattamuskeet Refuge is the **Swan**

© SARAH BRYAN

The Lodge at Lake Mattamuskeet was once the world's largest pumping station.

© SARAH BRYAN

A small snapping turtle puts on a threatening display near the Swan Quarter National Wildlife Refuge.

Quarter National Wildlife Refuge (252/926-4021, www.fws.gov/swanquarter), located along the north shore of the Pamlico Sound, and mostly accessible only by water. This too is a gorgeous waterscape full of wildlife.

GETTING THERE AND AROUND

This remote corner of North Carolina is crossed by two major north-south routes, U.S. 17 and U.S. 168, both coming down from Chesapeake, Virginia. U.S. 168 passes to the east, through Currituck, while U.S. 17 is the westerly route, closest to the Dismal Swamp and Elizabeth City, and passing through Edenton, Windsor,

and Williamston. At Williamston, U.S. 17 meets U.S. 64, a major east-west route that leads to Plymouth, Creswell, and Columbia, to the east.

If you keep going south on U.S. 17 from Williamston, the next major town you'll reach is Washington. From there you can turn east on U.S. 264 to reach Bath and Belhaven. Alternatively, you can reach U.S. 264 from the other direction, by picking up N.C. 94 at Columbia, and crossing Lake Mattamuskeet.

There is one state ferry route in this region, at the far northwest corner, between Currituck and Knotts Island (877/287-7488, free, 45 min.).

BEAUFORT AND THE CENTRAL COAST

Coming east from Raleigh towards the beaches and sounds of Carteret County, you'll start to feel the ocean when you're still many miles away from its shore. Somewhere between Kinston and New Bern, a good hour's drive from the Atlantic, the sky begins to expand in a way that suggests reflected expanses of water, like a mirage felt rather than seen. Getting closer to the coast, the pine forests on either side of the highway are peppered with mistletoe bundles. New Bern and Beaufort, centers of colonial commerce, connected North Carolina to the greater Atlantic world. Both towns are wonderfully preserved, ideal places for self-guided strolls with lots of window-shopping.

Below the crooked elbow of the Neuse River, the Croatan National Forest surrounds hidden lakes and tiny towns. To the northeast,

Cedar Island National Wildlife Refuge is a vast plain of marshes, gradually dropping off into Pamlico Sound. Cape Lookout National Seashore shelters the mainland from the ocean, a chain of barrier islands where a remote port, once one of the busiest maritime towns in North Carolina, and a whaling village, nearly washed away by a series of storms, now stand empty but for seagulls and ghosts.

You may hear folks in North Carolina refer to any point on the coast, be it Wilmington or Nags Head, as "Down East." In the most authentic, local usage of the term, Down East really refers to northeastern Carteret County, to the islands and marsh towns in a highly confined region along the banks of Core Sound, north of Beaufort. Like seemingly every scenic spot in North Carolina, Down

© HUGO WEBER JR / 123RF.COM

BEAUFORT

HIGHLIGHTS

◖ **Tryon Palace:** The splendid and, in its day, controversial seat of colonial government in North Carolina is reconstructed in New Bern's historic district, a significant destination worthy of a whole day's leisurely exploration (page 48).

◖ **North Carolina Maritime Museum:** North Carolina's seafaring heritage, in living traditions as well as history, is represented by fascinating exhibits and activities at this great museum (page 56).

◖ **Beaufort's Old Burying Ground:** Even if it weren't the final resting place of the "Little Girl Buried in a Barrel of Rum," this little churchyard would still be one of the prettiest and most interesting cemeteries in the South (page 57).

◖ **Core Sound Waterfowl Museum:** Actually a museum about people rather than ducks, the Waterfowl Museum eloquently tells of the everyday lives of past generations of Down Easterners, while bringing their descendants together to re-forge community bonds (page 62).

◖ **Cape Lookout National Seashore:** The more than 50 miles of coastline along Core and Shackleford Banks, now home to only wild horses and turtle nests, were once also the home of Bankers who made their livings in the fishing, whaling, and shipping trades (page 64).

◖ **North Carolina Aquarium:** Sharks and jellyfish and their aquatic kindred show their true beauty in underwater habitats at the aquarium, and trails and boat tours lead to the watery world outdoors (page 68).

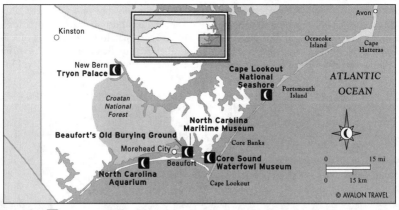

LOOK FOR ◖ TO FIND RECOMMENDED SIGHTS, ACTIVITIES, DINING, AND LODGING.

East communities are undergoing seismic cultural shifts as people "from off" move into the area, as young people leave home to make their lives and livings elsewhere, and as forces like global trade and environmental changes make the traditional maritime occupations of the region increasingly untenable. Nevertheless, Down Easterners fight to preserve the core treasures of Core Sound. Conservation and historic preservation efforts are underway, and they've already netted some victories. The best place to witness Down Easterners' passionate dedication to preserving their heritage is at the Core Sound Waterfowl Museum on Harkers Island. Members of the little communities along the sound have brought precious family

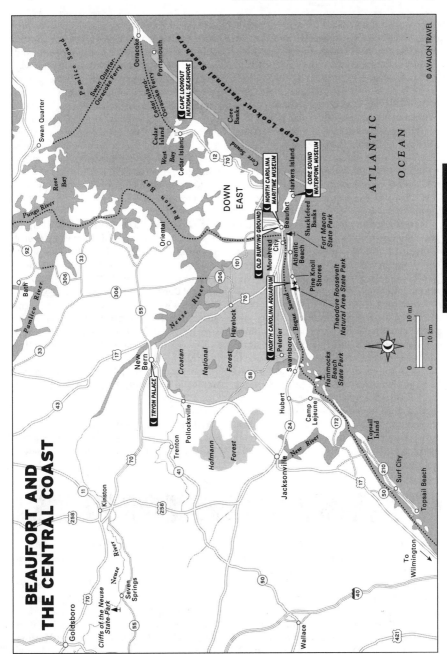

© AVALON TRAVEL

BEAUFORT

BEAUFORT AND THE CENTRAL COAST

Swan Quarter

Pamlico Sound

Swan Quarter-
Ocracoke Ferry

Ocracoke

Ocracoke

Portsmouth

Cedar Island-
Ocracoke Ferry

**CAPE LOOKOUT
NATIONAL SEASHORE**

Cape Lookout National Seashore

Core Banks

Cedar
Island

West
Bay

Cedar Island

12

70

Core Sound

ATLANTIC

OCEAN

Rose Bay

Pungo River

Raccoon Bay

DOWN
EAST

**NORTH CAROLINA
MARITIME MUSEUM**

Harkers Island

**CORE SOUND
WATERFOWL MUSEUM**

92

Oriental

Pamlico River

Bath

33

306

306

101

Neuse River

OLD BURYING GROUND

Beaufort

Morehead
City

Shackleford
Banks

Fort Macon
State Park

55

306

70

Havelock

NORTH CAROLINA AQUARIUM

Atlantic
Beach

Pine Knoll
Shores

Theodore Roosevelt
Natural Area State Park

33

17

New
Bern

Croatan

National

Forest

Peletier

Swansboro

Bogue Sound

58

10 mi

10 km

0

0

TRYON PALACE

43

Pollocksville

Hubert

Camp
Lejeune

Hammocks
Beach
State Park

41

Trenton

Hofmann

Forest

24

172

New River

Topsail
Island

11

70

Kinston

256

256

Jacksonville

17

50

210

Surf City

Goldsboro

70

Neuse River

Seven
Springs

Cliffs of the Neuse
State Park

55

50

40

Wallace

To
Wilmington

Topsail Beach

421

objects to be displayed at the museum, and the quilts, family photos, baseball uniforms, oyster knives, net hooks, and other treasures eloquently tell of their love of the water, the land, and each other.

PLANNING YOUR TIME

The standard beach-season rules apply to the coastal areas covered in this chapter. Lodging prices go up dramatically between Memorial Day and Labor Day, and though you might score a rock-bottom price if you visit on a mild weekend out of season, you might also find that some of the destinations you'd like to visit are closed.

North Carolina Sea Grant (www.ncsea grant.org, 919/515-2454) provides wallet cards listing the seasons for different seafood caught and served in Carteret County. The cards can be ordered by mail, or downloaded and printed from the website.

Late summer and early autumn are hurricane season all through the Southeast. Hurricane paths are unpredictable, so if you're planning a week on the beach, and know that a hurricane is hovering over Cuba, it won't necessarily hit North Carolina, though the central Carolina coast is always an odds-on favorite for landfall. Chances are you'll have pretty fair warning if a storm is coming—you won't wake up one morning to find your motel room windows covered with plywood, and everybody else in town gone—but it's always a good idea to familiarize yourself with evacuation routes, and

not take chances. A storm that's too far offshore to cause any weather problems can still mess up beach conditions, making waves and currents that are exciting for surfing but way too dangerous for swimming. (These caveats are relevant to the whole North Carolina coast, not just this region.)

Barring storms, the fall is a really beautiful time on the beaches here. The coastal weather is sometimes warm right into November, and though the water may be too chilly for swimming then, there's hardly a nicer time for walking tours of the old towns—except, of course, azalea season in the spring.

INFORMATION AND SERVICES

Hospitals in the area include **Carteret General Hospital** (3500 Arendell St., 252/808-6000, www.ccgh.org) in Morehead City (where the author was born), **Craven Regional Medical Center** (2000 Neuse Blvd., 252/633-8111, www.uhseast.com) in New Bern, **Duplin General Hospital** (401 North Main Street, 910/296-0941, www.uhseast.com) in Kenansville, **Lenoir Memorial Hospital** (100 Airport Rd., 252/522-7000, www.lenoir memorial.org) in Kinston, and **Wayne Memorial Hospital** (2700 Wayne Memorial Dr., 919/736-1110, www.waynehealth.org) in Goldsboro.

Extensive travel information is available from the **Crystal Coast Tourism Authority** (3409 Arendell St., 877/206-0929, www .crystalcoastnc.org).

New Bern

New Bern's history is understandably a great draw, and that, coupled with its beautiful natural setting at the confluence of the Neuse and Trent Rivers, makes it one of North Carolina's prime spots for tourism and retirement living. Despite the considerable traffic it draws, it is still a small and enormously pleasant city.

One all-important note: how to say it. It's your choice of "NYEW-bern" or "NOO-

bern"—and in some folks' accents it sounds almost like "Neighbor"—but never "New-BERN."

New Bern is easily reached, at the intersection of two major highways. U.S. 17 passes through New Bern going north-south, and U.S. 70 crosses east to west, with Beaufort and Morehead City to the east and Kinston to the west.

HISTORY

New Bern's early days were marked by tragedy. It was settled in 1710 by a community of Swiss and German colonists under the leadership of English surveyor John Lawson (author of the wonderful 1709 *A New Voyage to Carolina,* available today in reprint from the University of North Carolina Press), and Swiss entrepreneur Christoph von Graffenried (from Bern, of course). More than half of the settlers died en route to America, and those who made it across alive suffered tremendous hardship in their first months and years. Lawson and Graffenried were both captured in 1711 by the Tuscarora tribe, in one of the opening sallies of the Tuscarora War. Graffenried was released—according to some

accounts, because he wore such fancy clothes that the Tuscarora feared killing the governor. Lawson was burned at the stake, the first casualty of the Tuscarora War.

Despite early disaster, New Bern was on its feet again by the mid-18th century, at which time it was home to the colony's first newspaper, and its first chartered academy. It also became North Carolina's capital, an era symbolized by the splendor of Tryon Palace, one of the most recognizable architectural landmarks in North Carolina.

During the Civil War, New Bern was captured early by Ambrose Burnside's forces, and despite multiple Confederate attempts to retake the city, it remained a Union stronghold for the

© SARAH BRYAN

A monument honors the Confederate dead in one of New Bern's cemeteries.

balance of the war. It became a center for African American resistance and political organization through the Reconstruction years, a story grippingly told in historian David Cecelski's *The Waterman's Song* (also UNC Press).

SIGHTS
◖ Tryon Palace

Tryon Palace (610 Pollock St., 252/514-4956 or 252/514-4900, www.tryonpalace.org, 9 A.M.–5 P.M. Mon.–Sat., 1–5 P.M. Sun., last guided tour begins at 4 P.M., gardens open in the summer until 7 P.M., museum shop 9:30 A.M.–5:30 P.M. Mon.–Sat., 1–5:30 P.M. Sun.; $15 adults admission to all buildings and gardens, $6 grades 1–12; $8 adults admission just to gardens, kitchen office, blacksmith shop, and stables, $3 grades 1–12) is a rather remarkable feat of historic re-creation, a from-the-ground-up reconstruction of the 1770 colonial capitol and governor's mansion. Tryon Palace was a magnificent project the first time around too. Governor William Tryon bucked the preferences of Piedmont Carolinians, and

had his and the colonial government's new home built here in the coastal plain. He hired English architect John Hawks to design the complex, what would become a Georgian house upon an estate laid out in the Palladian style. The Palace's first incarnation was a fairly short one. It stood for a scant quarter-century before burning in 1798, and as the by-now state of North Carolina had relocated its governmental operations to Raleigh, there was no need to rebuild the New Bern estate.

It continued, however, to live on in Carolinians' imaginations for a century. In the early 20th century, a movement was afoot to rebuild Tryon Palace. By the 1950s, both the funds and, incredibly, John Hawks' original drawings and plans had been secured, and over a period of seven years the Palace was rebuilt. Today it's once again one of the most striking and recognizable buildings in North Carolina.

Tryon Palace is open for tours year-round, and it hosts many lectures and living history events throughout the year. One of the best times to visit is during the Christmas season, when not only is the estate decorated beautifully for the season, but they celebrate **Jonkonnu,** a colonial African American celebration that was once found throughout the Caribbean and Southeastern United States. For many generations it was celebrated in Eastern North Carolina, and here at Tryon Palace the tradition is recreated. At Jonkonnu—also called Junkanoo, John Canoe, and several other variations—African and African American slaves would put on a Mardi Gras–like frolic with deep African roots, parading through the plantation to music and wearing outlandish costumes, some representing folk characters associated with the celebration. It was a sort of upside-down day, when the social order was momentarily inverted, and the slaves could boldly walk right up onto the master's porch and demand gifts or money. Some whites got into the spirit of the celebration, and played along with this remarkable pantomime. It was a tradition fraught with both joy and sorrow, tapping into deeply volatile issues. Tryon Palace puts on a great recreation of Jonkonnu, one that's both lively and enlightening.

When you visit Tryon Palace, allow yourself plenty of time—a whole afternoon or even a full day. There are several buildings on the property where tours and activities are going on, the gardens are well worth seeing, and the surrounding neighborhood contains some wonderful old houses.

In the year 2010, in honor of New Bern's 300th anniversary, Tryon Palace plans to open the doors of its North Carolina History Education Center, an enormous new complex along the Trent River, next to the Tryon Palace gardens, with galleries, a performance hall, outdoor interpretive areas, and a great deal more.

New Bern Firemen's Museum

The New Bern Firemen's Museum (408 Hancock St., 252/636-4087, www.newbern museums.com, 10 A.M.–4 P.M. Mon.–Sat., $5 adults, $2.50 children) is a fun little museum—an idyll for the gearhead with an antiquarian bent. The museum houses a collection of 19th- and early 20th-century fire wagons and trucks, and chronicles the lively and contentious history of firefighting in New Bern. The city was the first in North Carolina, and one of the first in the country, to charter a fire department. After the Civil War, three fire companies operated here, one of which was founded before the War, and one founded during the Yankee occupation. (The third was a boys' bucket brigade, a sort of training program for junior firefighters.) During Reconstruction, every fire was occasion for a competition, as residents would gather around to see which company got to a blaze first—the good old boys or the carpetbaggers.

Attmore-Oliver House

The beautiful 1790 Attmore-Oliver House (510 Pollock St., 252/638-8558, www.newbern historical.org, hours and tour schedule vary, call for specifics, $4 adults, free for students) is a nice historic house museum, with exhibits about New Bern's very significant Civil War

history. It's also the headquarters of the New Bern Historical Society.

Birthplace of Pepsi

We often think of Coca-Cola as the quintessential Southern drink, but it was here in New Bern that Caleb Bradham, a drugstore owner, put together what he called Brad's Drink—later Pepsi-Cola. Pepsi-Cola Bottling Company operates a soda fountain and gift shop at the location of Bradham's pharmacy, called the Birthplace of Pepsi (256 Middle St., 252/636-5898, www.pepsistore.com).

ENTERTAINMENT AND EVENTS

New Bern's historic Harvey Mansion has a cozy old-fashioned pub in its cellar, the **1797 Steamer Bar** (221 S. Front St., 252/635-3232). As one would gather from its name, the pub serves steamed seafood and other light fare. **Captain Ratty's Seafood Restaurant** (202–206 Middle St., 800/633-5292 or 252/633-2088, www.captainrattys.com) also has a bar that's a popular gathering spot for locals and tourists alike.

SHOPPING

New Bern is a great place for antique shopping. The majority of the shops are within the 220–240 blocks of Middle Street. There are also periodic antique shows (and even a salvaged antique architectural hardware show) at the New Bern Convention Center. See www.visitnewbern.com for details.

Tryon Palace is a fun shopping spot for history buffs and home-and-garden fanciers. The historical site's **Museum Shop** (Jones House at Eden and Pollock Sts., 252/514-4932, 9:30 A.M.–5:30 P.M. Mon.–Sat., 1–5:30 P.M. Sun.) has a nice variety of books about history and architecture, as well as handcrafts and children's toy and games. The **Garden Shop** (610 Pollock St., 252/514-4932, 10 A.M.–5 P.M. Mon.–Sat., 1–5 P.M. Sun.) sells special bulbs and plants, when in season, grown in Tryon Palace's own greenhouse. Out of season you can still find a nice variety of gardening tools

BEAUFORT

BEAUFORT

and accessories. A Shop Pass is available at the Museum Shop; this allows you to visit the shops at Tryon Palace without paying the entrance fee.

SPORTS AND RECREATION

At New Bern's Sheraton Marina, **Barnacle Bob's Boat and Jet Ski Rentals** (100 Middle St., Dock F, 252/634-4100, www.boatand jetskinewbern.com, 9 A.M.–7 P.M. daily) rents one- and two-person Jet Skis ($65/hour, $45/half-hour) and 6–8-person pontoon boats ($65/hour, $220/4 hours, $420/8 hours).

ACCOMMODATIONS

The **☾ Aerie Bed and Breakfast** (509 Pollock St., 800/849-5553, www.aeriebedandbreakfast .com, $119–169) is the current incarnation of the 1880s Street-Ward residence. Its seven luxurious guest rooms are done up in Victorian furniture and earth-tone fabrics reflecting the house's earliest era. There is a lovely courtyard for guests to enjoy, and the inn is only one short block from Tryon Palace.

Also on Pollock Street, a few blocks away, are the **Harmony House Inn** (215 Pollock St., 800/636-3113, www.harmonyhouseinn .com, $99–175), the **Howard House Bed and Breakfast** (207 Pollock St., 252/514-6709, www.howardhousebnb.com, $89–149), and the **Meadows Inn** (212 Pollock St., 877/551-1776, www.meadowsinn-nc.com, $106–166). All three are appealing 19th-century houses decorated in the classic bed-and-breakfast style, and easy walking distance to Tryon Palace and to downtown.

Several motels can be found around New Bern as well, including **Holiday Inn Express** (3455 Martin Luther King Jr. Blvd., 877/863-4780, www.hiexpress.com, from around $100), and **Hampton Inn** (200 Hotel Dr., 252/637-2111, www.hamptoninn.com, from around $125).

Camping

New Bern's **KOA Campground** (1565 B St., 800/562-3341, www.newbernkoa.com) is just on the other side of the Neuse River from town, located right on the riverbank. Choices

include 20-, 30-, 40-amp RV sites; "kamping kabins and lodges"; and tent sites. Pets are allowed, and there is a dog park on-site. The campground is set up with free wireless Internet access, so you can check your email from a rental paddleboat, if you've a mind to. Stop by the New Bern Convention Center's tourist information center before checking in, and pick up a KOA brochure for some major coupons.

FOOD

The Italian restaurant **☾ Nikola's** (1503-A S. Glenburnie Rd., 252/638-6061, www .nikolasrestaurant.com, $15–25) is both very small and very popular, so reservations are recommended. Specialties include flounder stuffed with crabmeat, scallops, and shrimp, and Flounder Nikola's, filleted and laced with ham in white sauce; veal or chicken Romani sautéed in wine with mushrooms and artichoke hearts; and veal or chicken Fiorentina, with meat sauce, creamed spinach, and mozzarella served over pasta. Vegetarian entrées are all in the pasta category, but offer plenty of great options.

Down-home food choices include the **Country Biscuit Restaurant** (809 Broad St., 252/638-5151), which is open for breakfast, and is popular for, not surprisingly, its biscuits. **Moore's Olde Tyme Barbeque** (3711 Hwy. 17 S./Martin Luther King, Jr., Blvd., 252/638-3937, www.mooresbarbeque .com/Welcome.html) is a family business, in operation (at a series of different locations) since 1945. They roast and smoke their own barbeque in a pit on-site, burning wood that you'll see piled up by the shop. The menu is short and simple—featuring pork barbeque, chicken, shrimp, fish, hush puppies, fries, and slaw—and their prices are lower than many fast-food joints.

There are lots of good snack stops in New Bern, places to grab a bite or a cup of coffee before a day of touring on foot or on the water. The **Trent River Coffee Company** (208 Craven St., 252/514-2030, www.trentriver coffee.com) is a casual coffee shop in a cool old downtown storefront, and the coffee is good. It's sometimes patronized by well-behaved local dogs that lie under the tables patiently while their owners read the newspaper. This is a nice meeting place, and a dark oasis in the summer heat. **Port City Java** (323 Middle St., 252/633-7900, www.portcityjava.com) is an international chain, but it started in Wilmington, and has many locations on the North Carolina coast. The punch packed by Port City coffee is reliably good. One often stumbles upon cafés in communities where you wouldn't expect to be able to buy strong coffee, and it's at those times that a cup of espresso or a coffee shake is most appreciated. The **Cow Café** (319 Middle St., 252/672-9269) is a pleasant downtown creamery and snack shop with some homemade ice cream flavors you can't find anywhere else.

Croatan National Forest and Vicinity

A huge swath of swampy wilderness, the Croatan National Forest covers all the ground between the Neuse, Trent, and White Oak Rivers, and Bogue Sound, from New Bern to Morehead City and almost all the way to Jacksonville. Despite its size, Croatan is one of the lesser-known and less developed federal preserves in the state. The nearby towns (all three of them) of Jones County, population just over 10,000, enjoy a similar atmosphere of otherworldly sequestration, where barely traveled roads lead to dark expanses of forest and swamp, and old, narrow village streets.

CROATAN NATIONAL FOREST

Headquartered just off U.S. 70, south of New Bern, the Croatan National Forest (141 E. Fisher Ave., New Bern, 252/638-5628, http://ncnatural.com/NCUSFS/Croatan) has few established amenities for visitors, but plenty of land and water trails to explore.

BEAUFORT

Croatan National Forest, near Fisher's Landing, is a popular spot for alligators.

© SAMIR ARORA / DREAMSTIME.COM

Hiking

The main hiking route is the **Neusiok Trail,** which begins at the Newport River Parking area and ends at the Pinecliff Recreation Area on the Neuse, crossing 20 miles of beach, salt marsh, swamp, pocosin, and pinewoods. The 1.4-mile **Cedar Point Tideland Trail** covers estuary marshes and woods, starting at the Cedar Point boat ramp near Cape Carteret. The half-mile **Island Creek Forest Walk** passes through virgin hardwood forests and marl (compacted shell) outcroppings.

Boating

The park has designated the spectacular **Saltwater Adventure Trail.** This water route

---

JOHN LAWSON ON ALLIGATORS

Explorer John Lawson, in his *A New Voyage to Carolina*, describes a 1709 encounter with an alligator on the Neuse River.

The Allegator is the same, as the Crocodile, and differs only in Name. They frequent the sides of Rivers, in the Banks of which they make their Dwellings a great way under Ground . . . Here it is, that this amphibious Monster dwells all the Winter, sleeping away his time till the Spring appears, when he comes from his Cave, and daily swims up and down the Streams . . . This Animal, in these Parts, sometimes exceeds seventeen Foot long. It is impossible to kill them with a Gun, unless you chance to hit them about the Eyes, which is a much softer Place, than the rest of their impenetrable Armour. They roar, and make a hideous Noise against bad Weather, and before they come out of their Dens in the Spring. I was pretty much frightened with one of these once, which happened thus: I had built a House about half a Mile from an Indian Town, on the Fork of the Neus-River, where I dwelt by my self, excepting a young Indian Fellow, and a Bull-Dog, that I had along with me. I had not then been so long a Sojourner in America, as to be thoroughly acquainted with this Creature. One of them had got his Nest directly under my House, which stood on pretty high Land, and by a Creek-side, in whose Banks his Entring-place was, his Den reaching the Ground directly on which my House stood. I was sitting alone by the Fire-side (about nine a Clock at Night, some time in March) the Indian Fellow being gone to Town, to see his Relations; so that there was no

body in the House but my self and my Dog; when, all of a sudden, this ill-favour'd Neighbour of mine, set up such a Roaring, that he made the House shake about my Ears, and so continued, like a Bittern (but a hundred times louder, if possible), for four or five times. The Dog stared, as if he was frightened out of his Senses; nor indeed, could I imagine what it was, having never heard one of them before. Immediately I had another Lesson; and so a third. Being at that time amongst none but Savages, I began to suspect, that they were working some Piece of Conjuration under my House, to get away with my Goods . . . At last, my Man came in, to whom when I had told the Story, he laugh'd at me, and presently undeceiv'd me, by telling me what it was that made that Noise.

© SARAH BRYAN

(roughly 100 miles in length) starts at Brice's Creek south of New Bern, winds along north to the Neuse River, then follows the Neuse all the way to the crook at Harlowe, where it threads through the Harlowe Canal. The route then heads down to Beaufort and all the way through Bogue Sound, turning back inland on the White Oak River, and ending at Haywood Landing north of Swansboro. If you're up for the challenge, it's an incredible trip. For boat rentals, try **Brice's Creek Canoe Trails** (141 East Fisher Ave., New Bern, 252/636-6606).

Camping

Three campsites in the Croatan Forest are developed. **Neuse River** (also called Flanners Beach, $10–15) has 25 sites with showers and flush toilets. **Cedar Point** ($15), has 40 campsites with electricity, showers, and flush toilets. **Fisher's Landing** (free) has nine sites, but no facilities other than vault toilets. Primitive camping areas are at Great Lake, Catfish Lake, and Long Point.

TRENTON

A little ways outside of the Croatan National Forest is the very pretty village of Trenton. The Jones County seat's tiny, historic business district is an appropriate focal point for this bucolic area. A Revolutionary-era millpond, presided over by a large wooden mill, is a good picnic spot. It also makes for a nice destination for a short stroll after a meal at **Pop Tucci's** (141 W. Jones St., 252/448-1101) or the **Old Plant Diner** (346 W. Jones St., 252/448-1600). The 1880s board-and-batten Grace Episcopal Church sits next to a cemetery full of Victorian stones showing earthly chains rent asunder and heavenward-pointing hands.

KINSTON

The town of Kinston does not appear on many tourist maps, but those who overlook it are missing out. It's been through some rough years recently, especially due to the economic vacuum left by the vanishing tobacco industry, which for generations made Kinston quite a

KINSTON'S MUSIC LEGACY

Music has always been a big deal here, and African American Kinstonians have made immeasurable contributions to American music, from jazz to R&B to gospel. James Brown discovered what Kinston had to offer when, in Greensboro in 1964, he met and hired a talented young drummer and college student named Melvin Parker, a native of Kinston. Melvin accepted the job on the condition that Brown also hire his little brother – a saxophonist named Maceo. Melvin and Maceo Parker were not the only Kinstonians to tour with Brown's band. Band leader Nat Jones, trombonist Levi Raspberry, trumpeter Dick Knight, and quite a few other young men from this area made names for themselves and helped create the groundbreaking sound of funk. Plans are in the works to celebrate Kinston's African American musical history (and future). To find out if an event is planned for when you'll be in town, contact the **Kinston Community Council for the Arts** (400 N. Queen St., 252/527-2517, www.kinstoncca.com).

prosperous place. The town is very much alive, though, and interesting things are happening here, particularly in the arts and in historic preservation.

Sights

Like a lot of towns that were prosperous for many years and suddenly experienced a drying-up of funds, Kinston is an architectural time capsule. Driving (or better yet, walking) the several downtown blocks of **Queen Street**, the town's main artery, is an education in early 20th-century commercial architecture. The Hotel Kinston is the town's tallest building, an 11-story hotel with a ground level that's a crazy blend of Art Deco and Moorish motifs. The 1914 post office is a big, heavy beaux arts beauty, and the Queen Street Methodist Church is turreted within an inch of its life.

EARLY MENTAL INSTITUTIONS

Two of the state's most remarkable museums, both tiny and little-known, are located in Goldsboro and Kinston, about half an hour apart and an easy drive from Raleigh. They both display artifacts from the history of early mental institutions, from Cherry Hospital – formerly the state Asylum for the Colored Insane – in Goldsboro, and the Caswell Center, a residential home for the developmentally disabled in Kinston. These museums are not for the faint of heart; amid lists of accomplishments and milestones of medicine are hints and intimations of a tragic past, of suffering on an overwhelming scale and misguided early-20th-century attempts at progressive mental healthcare. Emblematic of these institutions' shared past is the fact that each museum has on display a cage, an early solution for controlling unruly patients.

Cherry Hospital is still a state-operated inpatient psychiatric hospital, located on the same grim, industrial-looking campus where the first patient was admitted in 1880. It was a segregated hospital, housing only African American patients, until 1965. The strikingly unselfconscious **Cherry Museum** focuses mainly on the history of the staff and the evolution of medical treatment at the facility, but among the displays one catches fleeting glimpses of what life may have been like here for the early patients. A framed page in one display case lists "Some Supposed Causes of Insanity in the Early Years," and among them are "religion," "jealousy," "hard study," "business trouble," "love affair," "pregnancy," "masturbation," "la grippe," "blow on head," and, most curious, simply "trouble." In a day when the definition of insanity was so all-encompassing, and, compounding the terror, African Americans had little or no legal recourse to protect themselves from false charges or incarceration, one can only imagine how many of the "insane" here were in fact healthy, lucid people who had fallen on hard times or committed some infraction of racial etiquette. In the earliest days, "therapy" consisted of work – picking crops in the fields, laboring in the laundry, or making bricks by the ton in the brickyard (which were then sold by the state for a profit). Clearly, such horrors as these are long behind us. They weren't confined to

The People's Bank building testifies to the heyday of early 20th-century African American commerce. With its many strange and daring experiments in building styles, Queen Street looks like a crazy quilt, but the buildings are beautifully complementary in their diversity. In the Herritage Street neighborhood, near the bend of the river, block upon block of grand old houses stand in threadbare glory, and on the other side of town, shotgun houses, that icon of Southern folk housing, line the alleys of the old working-class neighborhood.

The remains of the Confederate ironclad gunboat **CSS Neuse** are on display in Kinston, near the spot where she was scuttled in 1865 to keep her out of the hands of the advancing Union Army. All that remains is the core of the 158-foot-by-34-foot hull, but even in such deteriorated condition the *Neuse* is a striking feat of boatbuilding.

Entertainment and Events

Kinston is blessed with a great local arts engine, the **Kinston Community Council for the Arts** (400 N. Queen St., 252/527-2517, www.kinstoncca.com, 10 A.M.–6 P.M. Tues.–Fri., 10 A.M.–2 P.M. Sat.), which has the kind of energy and artistic vision one would expect to find in a much larger city. It occupies an old storefront on Queen Street, remodeled into a gorgeous gallery and studio space. In addition to the many community events that are hosted here, KCCA has consistently innovative exhibits in the main gallery. From avant-garde photography and collage to a recent exhibition of dozens of custom motorcycles, the Kinston Arts Council is a significant and provocative art space.

Sports and Recreation

The **Kinston Indians,** an old baseball team

Cherry Hospital at the time, and certainly don't occur here today, but the grief of the tens of thousands of people who lived here in the early 1900s hangs heavy in the air.

To visit Cherry Museum, you must enter the campus of Cherry Hospital (201 Stevens Mill Rd., Goldsboro, 919/731-3417, www.cherryhospital.org), on Highway 581, near I-70 and U.S. 117, outside of Goldsboro. (You'll see a sign on I-70.) Once on campus, follow the signs to the museum. Once there, you must ring the doorbell and wait to be admitted. The public is admitted 8 A.M.-5 P.M. Monday-Friday.

Down the road in Kinston, about half an hour east, you'll find the **Caswell Center Museum and Visitors Center.** The Caswell Center admitted its first patients in 1914 as the Caswell School for the Feeble Minded. Like Cherry Hospital, the Caswell Center is still an active inpatient facility, and it is nothing like the bleak place documented in the museum's displays about the first years here. But this too is an eye-opening education in early attitudes towards mental healthcare. The Caswell Center's museum is more blunt in its presentation than the delicate Cherry Museum, confronting directly the sad facts of its history by exhibiting objects like the combination straight-jacket-rompers that the earliest patients had to wear, and addressing the Depression-era overcrowding and lack of food. Though the Caswell Center's patients were all white until the era of integration, they were like the residents of the Asylum for the Colored Insane in that among their ranks were mentally healthy people – unwed mothers, people with physical handicaps, juvenile delinquents – who were crowded into dormitories with the patients who did suffer from mental handicaps. An articulate love letter written from one patient, clearly not disabled, to another hints at the bizarre contradictions of life in an early mental institution.

The Caswell Center Museum and Visitors Center (2415 W. Vernon Ave., Kinston, 252/208-3780, www.caswellcenter.org) is open 8 A.M.-5 P.M. Monday-Friday and other times by appointment.

Both museums are free, but please make a donation to help ensure that their amazing stories will continue to be told.

who are nowadays a Class-A affiliate of the Cleveland Indians, play their home games at historic **Grainger Stadium.** Grainger is a homey 1949 field, the second-oldest in the Carolina League. There's nothing like a baseball game in a small town that really, really cares, and baseball ranks nearly as high as music on the list of Kinstonians' favorite things. At a memorable weekday afternoon Indians game in a recent season, the opening pitch was delayed when the stadium's PA system malfunctioned and failed to play the recording of the national anthem. After a few impatient moments, a loud-voiced man in the crowd began singing. The rest of the crowd joined him at "can you see" and sang the anthem all the way through (staying on pitch right through the high note—this is a musical town). When the singing was over, the players turned their backs to the flag just long enough to applaud the crowd, before they took the field and played ball.

Accommodations and Food

Several chain motels are located just outside of the downtown area. The **Hampton Inn** (1382 U.S. 258 S., 252/523-1400, www.hamptoninn .com, around $85) is convenient and comfortable, and the staff are especially nice.

There are quite a few good places to eat in Kinston. The best bet for a quick and tasty sandwich is the **Peach House** (412 W. Vernon Ave., 252/522-2526). For Carolina barbecue, **King's BBQ** (405 E. New Bern Rd., 800/332-6465, www.kingsbbq.com) has been a local favorite for more than 60 years. You'll see billboards throughout the area for their "Famous Pig in a Puppy," pork barbecue baked into a hush puppy sandwich. They also hit the nail on the head with their Brunswick stew, fried chicken, fried sea trout, and "banana pudding in an edible waffle bowl." King's also does a mail-order business in hand-chopped pork barbecue for $8 a pound.

SEVEN SPRINGS

Seven Springs is an attractive, historic little town about half an hour southwest of Kinston. It's the site of **Cliffs of the Neuse State Park** (345-A Park Entrance Rd., Seven Springs, 919/778-6234, www.ncparks.gov/Visit/parks/clne/main.php, park office open 8 A.M.–5 P.M. weekdays, park open 8 A.M.–6 P.M. Nov.–Feb., 8 A.M.–8 P.M. Apr.–May, 8 A.M.–9 P.M. June–Aug., 8 A.M.–8 P.M. Sept. and Oct.), a highly unusual blend of environments, including high red bluffs overlooking the Neuse River, hardwood and pine forests, and cypress swamps. Hiking trails follow the cliff line through Spanish moss-draped forests. Boating and swimming are permitted at the park's manmade lake between Memorial Day and Labor Day, 10 A.M.–5:45 P.M., swimming only when a lifeguard is on duty. Boats must be rented—no private watercraft are permitted. Camping is available between March 15 and November 30. There is a washhouse with hot showers and electricity, and several water stations are located in the campsite. Take note that, unless you have a medical emergency, you must stay inside the park from the time the gates close until 8 A.M. the next morning—so no slipping out for a late supper.

Beaufort and Vicinity

It's an oft-cited case of the perversity of Southern speech that Beaufort, North Carolina, receives the French treatment of "eau"—so it's pronounced "BO-furt"—whereas Beaufort, South Carolina, a rather similar Lowcountry port town south of Charleston, is pronounced "Byew-furt."

The third-oldest town in North Carolina, Beaufort holds its own with its elders, Bath and New Bern, in the pretty department. The little port was once North Carolina's window on the world, a rather cosmopolitan place that sometimes received news from London or Barbados sooner than from Raleigh. The streets are crowded with extremely beautiful old houses, many built in a double-porch, steep-roofed style that shows off the early citizenry's cultural ties to the wider Caribbean and Atlantic world.

In the late 1990s, a shipwreck was found in Beaufort Inlet that is believed to be that of the *Queen Anne's Revenge,* a French slaver captured by the pirate Blackbeard in 1717 to be the flagship of his unsavory fleet. He increased its arsenal to 40 cannons, but it was nevertheless sunk in the summer of 1718. Blackbeard himself was killed at Ocracoke Inlet a few months later, and it took five musketballs and 40 sword wounds to finish him off. His body was dumped overboard, but his head carried on its master's infamous career a little longer, scaring folks from atop a pike in Virginia. Incredibly cool artifacts from the *QAR* keep emerging from the waters of the inlet. Beaufort had been a favorite haunt of Blackbeard's, and you can find out all about him at the North Carolina Maritime Museum.

From the Maritime Museum, it's just a few steps to Beaufort's cafés, antique shops, and docks, clustered along Front Street. From the docks you can see Carrot Island, with its herd of wild horses, one of the last in eastern North Carolina, and you can catch a ride on a ferry or tour boat to cross the sound to the Cape Lookout National Seashore, or get a close-up glimpse of wildlife in the surrounding salt marshes.

SIGHTS
(North Carolina Maritime Museum

The North Carolina Maritime Museum (315

Front St., 252/728-7317, www.ah.dcr.state
.nc.us/sections/maritime/, 9 A.M.–5 P.M. Mon.–
Fri., 10 A.M.–5 P.M. Sat., 1–5 P.M. Sun., free) is
among the best museums in the state. Even if
you don't think you're interested in boatbuilding or maritime history, you'll get caught up
in the exhibits here. Historic watercraft and
reconstructions and models of boats are on display, well presented in rich historical and cultural context. There's also a lot to learn about
the state's fishing history—not only pertaining to the fisheries themselves, but also to related occupations, such as the highly complex
skill of net-hanging. Far from being limited to
the few species of catches of today's fisheries,
early North Carolina seamen also carried on
a big business hunting sea turtles, porpoises,
and even whales.

Across the street from the museum's main
building, perched on the dock, is the **Harvey
W. Smith Watercraft Center.** North Carolina
mariners had for many generations an international reputation as expert shipbuilders, and
even today, some builders continue to construct
large, seaworthy vessels in their own backyards.

This has always been done "by the rack of the
eye," as they say here, which means that the
builders use traditional knowledge handed
down over the generations, rather than modern industrial methods. Their exceptional ex-
pertise is beautifully demonstrated by the craft
in the museum and by boats still working the
waters today. Here at the Watercraft Center,
the Maritime Museum provides workspace
for builders of full-size and model boats, and
it teaches a vast array of classes in boatbuilding skills, both traditional and mechanized
methods.

◖ Old Burying Ground

One of the most beautiful places in all of North
Carolina, Beaufort's Old Burying Ground
(Anne St., open daylight hours daily) is as picturesque a cemetery as you'd ever want to be
buried in. It's quite small by the standards of
some old Carolina towns, and crowded with
18th- and 19th-century stones. Huge old live
oaks, Spanish moss, wisteria, and resurrection
ferns, which unfurl and turn green after a rain-
storm, give the Burying Ground an irresistibly

© SARAH BRYAN

The Old Burying Ground has a gothic feel and reflects the seafaring history of Beaufort.

BEAUFORT

gothic feel. Many of the headstones reflect the maritime heritage of this town, such as that of a sea captain whose epitaph reads, "The form that fills this silent grave/once tossed on ocean's rolling wave/but in a port securely fast/ he's dropped his anchor here at last."

Captain Otway Burns, an early privateer who spent much time in Beaufort, is buried here; his grave is easy to spot, as it is topped by a canon from his ship, the *Snap Dragon*. Nearby is another of the graveyard's famous burials, that of the "Little Girl Buried in a Barrel of Rum." This unfortunate waif is said to have died at sea and been placed in a cask of rum, to preserve her body for burial on land. Visitors often bring toys and trinkets to leave on her grave, which is marked by a simple wooden plank. Though hers is the most gaudily festooned, you'll see evidence of this old tradition of funerary gifts on other graves here as well—most often, in this cemetery, coins and shells. This is a tradition found throughout the coastal South and the Caribbean, with roots tracing back to Africa. Feel free to add to her haul of goodies, but it's not karmically advisable to tamper with those already there.

BLACKBEARD AND BONNET: THE BOYS OF 1718

In the 18th century, the Carolina coast was positively verminous with pirates. For the most part they hung out around Charleston Harbor, like a bunch of rowdies on a frat house balcony, causing headaches for passers-by. Some liked to venture up the coast, however, into the inlets and sounds of North Carolina. Our most famous pirate guests were Blackbeard, whose real name was **Edward Teach,** and **Stede Bonnet.** They did most of their misbehaving in our waters during the year 1718.

Blackbeard is said never to have killed a man except in self-defense, but clearly he was so bad he didn't need to kill to make his badness known. He was a huge man with a beard that covered most of his face, and his hair is usually depicted twisted up into ferocious dreadlocks. He wore a bright red coat and festooned himself with every weapon small enough to carry; and as if all that didn't make him scary enough, he liked to wear burning cannon fuses tucked under the brim of his hat. He caused trouble from the Bahamas to Virginia, taking ships, treasure, and child brides as fancy led him.

Poor Stede Bonnet. With a name like that, he should have known better than to try to make a living intimidating people. He is said to have been something of a fancy-pants, a man with wealth, education, and a nagging wife. To get away from his better half, he bought a ship, hired a crew, and set sail for a life of crime. Though never quite as tough as Blackbeard, with whom he was briefly partners, Bonnet caused enough trouble along the Southern coast that the gentlemen of Charleston saw to it that he was captured and hanged. Meanwhile, the Virginia nabobs had also had it with Blackbeard's interference in coastal commerce, and Governor Spottswood dispatched his men to kill him. This they did at Ocracoke, but it wasn't easy; even after they shot, stabbed, and beheaded Blackbeard, his body taunted them by swimming laps around the ship before finally giving up the ghost.

Blackbeard has in effect surfaced again. In 1996, a ship was found off the North Carolina coast that was identified as Blackbeard's flagship, the *Queen Anne's Revenge.* All manner of intriguing artifacts have been brought up from the ocean floor: cannons and blunderbuss parts, early hand grenades, even a penis syringe supposed to have been used by the syphilitic pirates to inject themselves with mercury. (During one standoff in Charleston Harbor, Blackbeard and his men took hostages to ransom for medical supplies. Perhaps this explains why they were so desperate.) To view artifacts and learn more about Blackbeard, Stede Bonnet, and their lowdown ways, visit the North Carolina Maritime Museum in Beaufort and in Southport, as well as the websites of the *Queen Anne's Revenge* (www.qaronline .com) and the Office of State Archaeology (www.arch.dcr.state.nc.us).

Beaufort Historic Site

The Beaufort Historic Site (130 Turner St., 252/728-5225, www.beauforthistoricsite.org, $8 adults, $4 children) recreates life in late 18th- and early 19th-century Beaufort in several restored historic buildings. The 1770s "jump-and-a-half" (1.5-story) Leffers Cottage reflects middle-class life in its day, as a merchant, whaler, or—in this case—schoolmaster would have lived it. The Josiah Bell and John Manson Houses, both from the 1820s, reflect the graceful Caribbean-influenced architecture so prevalent in the early days of the coastal South. A restored apothecary shop, 1790s wooden courthouse, and a haunted 1820s jail that was used into the 1950s, are among the other important structures here. There are tours led by costumed interpreters, as well as driving tours of the old town in double-decker buses. Hours vary by season: 9:30 A.M.–5 P.M. Monday–Saturday March 1–November 31, plus 1–4 P.M. Sundays in June–August; 10 A.M.–4 P.M. Monday–Saturday December 1–February 28.

SPORTS AND RECREATION
Diving

North Carolina's coast is a surprisingly good place for diving. The **Discovery Diving Company** (414 Orange St., 252/728-2265, www.discoverydiving.com, $65–110/excursion) leads half- and full-day diving trips to explore the reefs and dozens of fascinating shipwrecks that lie at the bottom of the sounds and ocean near Beaufort.

Cruises and Wildlife Tours

Coastal Ecology Tours (252/247-3860, www.goodfortunesails.com, prices vary) runs very special tours on the *Good Fortune* of the Cape Lookout National Seashore and other island locations in the area, as well as a variety of half-day, day-long, overnight, and short trips, to snorkel, shell, kayak, and watch birds, and cruises to Morehead City restaurants, and other educational and fun trips. Prices range from $40 per person for a 2.5-hour dolphin-watching tour to $600 a night plus meals for an off-season overnight boat rental.

Lookout Cruises (600 Front St., 252/504-7245, www.lookoutcruises.com) carries sightseers on lovely catamaran rides in the Beaufort and Core Sound region, out to Cape Lookout, and on morning dolphin-watching trips.

Island Ferry Adventures (610 Front St., 252/728-7555, www.islandferryadventures.com, $10–15 adults, $5–8 children) runs dolphin-watching tours, trips to collect shells at Cape Lookout, and trips to see the wild ponies of Shackleford Banks.

Mystery Tours (600 Front St., 252/728-7827 or 866/230-2628, www.mysteryboattours.com, $15–50 adults, free–$25 children, some cruises for grownups only) offers harbor tours and dolphin-watching trips, as well as a variety of brunch, lunch, and dinner cruises, and trips to wild islands where children can hunt for treasure.

ACCOMMODATIONS

◖ **Outer Banks Houseboats** (324 Front St., 252/728-4129, www.outerbankshouseboats.com) will rent you your own floating vacation home, drive it for you to a scenic spot, anchor it, and then come and check in on you every day during your stay. You'll have a skiff for your own use, but you may just want to lie on the deck all day and soak up the peacefulness. Rates run from $1,200 per weekend for the smaller houseboat, to $3,000 per week for the luxury boat, with plenty of rental options in between.

The **Inlet Inn** (601 Front St., 800/554-5466, www.inlet-inn.com) has one of the best locations in town, right on the water, near the docks where many of the ferry and tour boats land. If planning to go dolphin-watching or hop the ferry to Cape Lookout, you can get ready at a leisurely pace, and just step outside to the docks. Even in the high season, prices are quite reasonable.

The **Beaufort Inn** (101 Ann St., 252/728-2600, www.beaufort-inn.com) is a large hotel on Gallants Channel, along one side of the colonial district. It's an easy walk to the main downtown attractions, and the hotel's outdoor hot tub and balconies with great views make it tempting to stay in as well. The **Pecan Tree Inn** (116 Queen St., 800/728-7871, www.pecan tree.com) is such a grand establishment that the town threw a parade in honor of the laying of its cornerstone in 1866. The house is still splendid, as are the 5,000-square-foot gardens. Catty-corner to the Old Burying Grounds is the **Langdon House Bed and Breakfast** (135 Craven St., 252/728-5499, www.langdon house.com). One of the oldest buildings in town, this gorgeous house was built in the 1730s on a foundation of English ballast stones.

FOOD

Among the Beaufort eateries certified by Carteret Catch as serving local seafood are the **Blue Moon Bistro** (119 Queen St., 252/728-5800, www.bluemoonbistro.biz), **Sharpie's Grill and Bar** (521 Front St., 252/838-0101, www.sharpiesgrill.com), and **Aqua Restaurant** (114 Middle Ln. "behind Clawsons," 252/728-7777, www.aquaexperience.com).

If you're traveling with a cooler and want to buy some local seafood to take home, try the **Fishtowne Seafood Center** (100 Wellons Dr., 252/728-6644) or **Tripps Seafood** (1224 Harkers Island Rd., 252/447-7700).

◖ **Beaufort Grocery** (117 Queen St., 252/728-3899, www.beaufortgrocery.com, open for lunch and dinner every day but Tues., brunch on Sun., $20–36) is, despite its humble name, a sophisticated little eatery. At lunch it serves salads and crusty sandwiches, along with "Damn Good Gumbo" and specialty soups. In the evening the café atmosphere gives way to that of a more formal gourmet dining room. Some of the best entrées include boneless chicken breast sautéed with pecans in a hazelnut cream sauce; Thai-rubbed roast half duckling; and whole baby rack of lamb, served with garlic mashed potatoes, tortillas, and a margarita-chipotle sauce. Try the cheesecake for dessert.

The waterfront **Front Street Grill** (300 Front St., 252/728-4956, www.frontstreet grillatstillwater.com) is popular with boaters drifting through the area, as well as diners who arrive by land. The emphasis is on seafood and fresh regional ingredients. Front Street Grill's

wine list is extensive, and they have repeatedly won *Wine Spectator* magazine's Award of Excellence.

Aqua (114 Middle Ln., 252/728-7777, www.aquaexperience.com, Tues.–Thurs. dinner at 6 P.M., Fri. and Sat. dinner at 5:30 P.M., small plates $8–14, big plates $23–28) divides its menu into "small plates" and "big plates," so you can make up a dinner tapas-style and sample more of the menu. The fare ranges from Southern classics like shrimp and grits to more exotic fare like a Japanese bento box with yellow fin tuna, calamari, and shrimp spring rolls. Vegetarians will find limited options, but if you're looking for local seafood, you're in luck.

MOREHEAD CITY

Giovanni da Verrazano may have been the first European to set foot in present-day Morehead City when he sailed into Bogue Inlet. It wasn't until the mid-19th century that the town actually came into being, built as the terminus of the North Carolina Railroad to connect the state's overland commerce to the sea. Despite its late start, Morehead City has been a busy place. During the Civil War it was the site of major encampments by both armies. A series of horrible hurricanes in the 1890s, culminating in 1899's San Ciriaco Hurricane, brought hundreds of refugees from the towns along what is now the Cape Lookout National Seashore. They settled in a neighborhood that they called Promise Land, and many of their descendants are still here.

The Atlantic and North Carolina Railroad operated a large hotel here in the 1880s, ushering in Morehead's role as a tourist spot, and the bridge to the Bogue Banks a few decades later increased holiday traffic considerably.

Morehead is also an official state port, one of the best deepwater harbors on the Atlantic Coast. This admixture of tourism and gritty commerce gives Morehead City a likeable, real-life feel missing in many coastal towns today.

Sights

Morehead City's history is on display at **The**

History Place (1008 Arendell St., 252/247-7533, www.thehistoryplace.org, 10 A.M.–4 P.M. Tues.–Sat.). There are many interesting and eye-catching historical artifacts on display, but the most striking exhibit is that of a carriage, clothes, and other items pertaining to Emeline Pigott, Morehead City's Confederate heroine. She was a busy girl all through the Civil War, working as a nurse, a spy, and a smuggler. The day she was captured, she was carrying 30 pounds of contraband hidden in her skirts, including Union troop movement plans, a collection of gloves, several dozen skeins of silk, needles, toothbrushes, a pair of boots, and five pounds of candy.

Entertainment and Events

Seafood is a serious art here. North Carolina's second-largest festival takes place in Morehead City every October, the enormous **North Carolina Seafood Festival** (252/726-6273, www.ncseafoodfestival.org). The city's streets shut down and over 150,000 visitors descend on the waterfront. Festivities kick off with a blessing of the fleet, followed with music, fireworks, competitions (like the flounder-toss), and, of course, lots and lots of food.

If you're in the area on the right weekend in November, you'll not want to deprive yourself of the gluttonous splendor of the **Mill Creek Oyster Festival** (Mill Creek Volunteer Fire Department, 2370 Mill Creek Rd., Mill Creek, 252/247-4777). Food, and lots of it, is the focus of this event. It's a small-town fête, a benefit for the local volunteer fire department, and the meals are cooked by local experts. You'll be able to choose from all-you-can-eat roasted oysters, fried shrimp, fried spot (a local fish), and more, all in mass quantities. The oysters may not be local these days (and few served on this coast are), but the cooking is very local—an authentic taste of one of North Carolina's best culinary traditions. Mill Creek is northwest of Morehead City on the Newport River.

Sports and Recreation

Many of this region's most important historic and natural sites are underwater. From Morehead City's **Olympus Dive Center** (713 Shepard St., 252/726-9432, www.olympus diving.com), divers of all levels of experience can take charter trips to dozens of natural and artificial reefs that teem with fish, including the ferocious-looking but not terribly dangerous eight-foot-long sand tiger shark. There are at least as many amazing shipwrecks to choose from, including an 18th-century schooner, a luxury liner, a German U-boat, and many Allied commercial and military ships that fell victim to the U-boats that infested this coast during World War II.

Food

The **Sanitary Fish Market** (501 Evans St., 252/247-3111, www.sanitaryfishmarket.com) is probably Morehead City's best-known institution. The rather odd name reflects its 1930s origins as a seafood market that was bound by its lease and its fastidious landlord to be kept as clean as possible. Today it's a huge family seafood restaurant. Long lines in season and on weekends demonstrate its popularity. Of particular note are its famous hush puppies, which have a well-deserved reputation as some of the best in the state. Be sure to buy a Sanitary t-shirt on the way out; it'll help you blend in everywhere else in the state.

The **Bistro-by-the-Sea** (4031 Arendell St., 252/247-2777, www.bistro-by-the-sea.com, 5–9:30 P.M. Tues.–Thurs., 5–10 P.M. Fri. and Sat., entrées $10–25) participates in Carteret Catch, a program that brings together local fishermen with restaurants, fish markets, and wholesalers, to ensure that fresh locally caught seafood graces the tables of Carteret County. In addition to seafood, steak, tenderloin, and prime rib are specialties here.

Café Zito (105 S. 11th St., 252/726-6676, www.cafezito.com, dinner beginning at 5:30 P.M. Fri.–Mon., closed Tues.–Thurs., entrées $17–27), located in a pretty 1898 house, serves elegant Mediterranean fare, and also participates in Carteret Catch.

Captain Bill's (701 Evans St., 252/726-2166, www.captbills.com) is Morehead City's oldest restaurant, founded in 1938. Try the conch stew, and be sure to visit the otters that live at the dock outside. Another famous eating joint in Morehead City is **El's Drive-In** (3706 Arendell St., 252/726-3002), a tiny place across from Carteret Community College. El's has been around almost as many forevers as the Sanitary. It's most famous for its shrimp burgers, but serves all sorts of fried delights. **Mrs. Willis' Restaurant** (3114 Bridges St., 252/726-3741, www.mrswillisrestaurant .com) is a popular home-style lunch and dinner spot. It's a sit-down restaurant, certainly not as casual as El's, but plenty laid-back just the same. Charcoal-grilled steaks are the specialty. **Cox Family Restaurant** (4109 Arendell St., 252/726-6961) also has served down-home cooking for many years, and is known for its friendly staff and coterie of local regulars.

For an old fashioned ladies' luncheon or afternoon tea, visit the tiny, five-table tearoom at the **Tea Clipper** (The History Place, 1012 Arendell St., 252/240-2800, www.thetea clipper.com, 11 A.M.–5 P.M. Tues.–Sat.). In addition to the many teas, you can order scones and desserts, and dainty quiche and sandwiches. The Tea Clipper shop, the mother ship of the little tearoom, has more than 120 teas of all kinds sold by the scoop.

HARKERS ISLAND

The Core Sound region, which stretches to the east-northeast of Beaufort many miles up to the Pamlico Sound, is a region of birds and boats. Like much of the Carolina coast, the marshes and pocosins here are visited by countless flocks of migratory birds on their ways to and from their winter quarters, as well as the many birds that live here year-round. Consequently, hunting has always been a way of life here, almost as much as fishing. In earlier generations (and to a much lesser extent today), men who fished most of the year did a sideline business in bird hunting; not only would they eat the birds they shot, but they made money selling feathers for ladies' hats, they trained bird dogs for their own and other hunters' use, and they served as guides to visiting hunters. Many Down Easterners also became expert

decoy carvers. This art survives today, partly as art for art's sake, and also for its original purpose. Woodworking on a much grander scale has also defined the culture of this section, as it has bred generations of great boat-builders. Keep an eye out as you drive through Harkers Island, because you may see boats under construction in folks' backyards—not canoes or dinghies, but full-sized fishing boats.

To get to Harkers Island, follow U.S. 70 east from Beaufort, around the dogleg that skirts the North River. A little east of the town of Otway you'll see Harkers Island Road. Take a right on Harkers Island Road, and head south towards Straits. Straits Road will take you through the town by the same name, and then across a bridge over the Straits themselves, finally ending up on Harkers Island.

◖ Core Sound Waterfowl Museum

The Core Sound Waterfowl Museum (1785 Island Rd., Harkers Island, 252/728-1500, www.coresound.com, 10 A.M.–5 P.M. Mon.–Sat., 2–5 P.M. Sun., free), which occupies a beautiful modern building on Shell Point, next to the Cape Lookout National Seashore headquarters, is a community labor of love. The museum is home to exhibits crafted by members of the communities represented, depicting the Down East maritime life through decoys, nets, and other tools of the trades, everyday household objects, beautiful quilts and other utilitarian folk arts, and lots of other things held dear by the people who live and lived here. This is a sophisticated, modern institution, but its community roots are evident in touching details like the index-card labels, written in the careful script of elderly ladies, explaining what certain objects are, what they were used for, and who made them. For instance, just as Piedmont textile workers made and treasured their loom hooks, folks down here took pride in the hooks that they made to assist in the perennial off-season work of hanging nets. Baseball uniforms on display represent an era when one town's team might have to travel by ferry to its opponent's field. The museum hosts monthly get-togethers for members of communities Down East, a different town every month, which are like old home days. Families and long-lost friends reunite over home-cooked food, to reminisce about community history and talk about their hopes and concerns for the future.

The museum's gift shop has a nice selection of books and other items related to Down East culture. Be sure to pick up a copy of *The Harkers Island Cookbook* by the Harkers Island United Methodist Women. This cookbook has become a regional classic for its wonderful blend of authentic family recipes and community stories. You might also be able to find a Core Sound Christmas Tree, made by Harvey and Sons in nearby Davis. This old family fishery has made a hit in recent years manufacturing small Christmas trees out of recycled crab pots. It's a whimsical item, but it carries deep messages about the past and future of the Core Sound region.

Core Sound Decoy Carvers Guild

Twenty years ago, some decoy-carving friends Down East decided over a pot of stewed clams to found the Core Sound Decoy Carvers Guild (1575 Harkers Island Rd., 252/838-8818, www .decoyguild.com, call for hours). The Guild, which is open to the public, gives demonstrations, competitions, and classes for grown-ups and children, and has a museum shop that's a nice place to browse.

Events

The Core Sound Decoy Carvers Guild also hosts the **Core Sound Decoy Festival,** usually held in the early winter. Several thousand people come to this annual event—more than the number of permanent residents on Harkers Island—to buy, swap, and teach the art of making decoys.

Food

Captain's Choice Restaurant (977 Island Rd., 252/728-7122) is a great place to try traditional Down East chowder. Usually made of clams, but sometimes with other shellfish or fish, chowder in Carteret County is a point of pride. The point is the flavor of the seafood itself, which must be extremely fresh, and not hidden behind lots of milk and spices. Captain's Choice serves chowder in the old-time way—with dumplings.

VILLAGE OF CEDAR ISLAND

For a beautiful afternoon's drive, head back to the mainland, and follow U.S. 70 north. You'll go through some tiny communities—Williston, Davis, Stacy—and, if you keep bearing north on Highway 12 when U.S. 70 heads south to the town of Atlantic, you'll eventually reach the tip of the peninsula, and the fishing village of Cedar Island. This little fishing town has the amazing ambience of being at the end of the earth. From the peninsula's shore you can barely see land across the sounds. The ferry to Ocracoke departs from Cedar Island, and it's an unbelievable two-hours-plus ride across the Pamlico Sound to get there. The beach here is absolutely gorgeous, and horses roam. They're not the famous wild horses of the Outer Banks, but they move about freely as if they were.

A spectacular location for bird-watching is the **Cedar Island National Wildlife Refuge** (on U.S. 70, east of the town Atlantic, 252/926-4021, www.fws.gov/cedarisland). Nearly all of its 14,500 acres are brackish marshland, and it's often visited in season by redhead ducks, buffleheads, surf scoters, and many other species. While there are trails for hiking and biking, this refuge is primarily intended as a safe haven for the birds.

Accommodations and Food

⟨ The Driftwood Motel (3575 Cedar Island Rd., 252/225-4861, www.clis.com/deg/drift2 .htm) is a simple motel in an incredible location, and since the ferry leaves from its parking lot, it's the place to stay if you're coming from or going to Ocracoke. There's also camping here, for $16 per tent and $18–20 for RV, with electricity, water, and sewer.

The Driftwood's **Pirate's Chest Restaurant** is the only restaurant on Cedar Island, so it's a good thing that it's a good one. Local seafood is the specialty, and dishes can be adapted for vegetarians.

GETTING THERE AND AROUND

By Car

One of the state's main east–west routes, U.S. 70, gives easy access to almost all of the destinations in this chapter. From Raleigh to Beaufort is a distance of a little over 150 miles, but keep in mind that large stretches of the highway are in commercial areas with plenty of traffic and red lights. U.S. 70 continues past Beaufort, snaking up along Core Sound through little Down East towns like Otway and Davis, finally petering out in the town of Atlantic. At Sea Level, Highway 13 branches to the north, across the Cedar Island Wildlife Refuge and ending at the Cedar Island–Ocracoke Ferry.

Down south, to reach the Bogue Banks (Atlantic Beach, Emerald Isle, and neighboring beaches) by road, bridges cross Bogue Sound on Highway 58 at both Morehead City and Cedar Point (not to be confused with Cedar Island).

By Ferry

Ferry service between Carteret County (Beaufort, Morehead City, Harkers Island, Cedar Point) and Cape Lookout National Seashore is detailed in the Cape Lookout section, later in this chapter. Inland, a 20-minute free passenger ferry **crosses the Neuse River** between Cherry Branch (near Cherry Point) and Minesott Beach in Pamlico County every half-hour (vehicles and passengers, pets allowed, 800/339-9156).

Lower Outer Banks

The southern reaches of the Outer Banks of North Carolina comprise some of the region's most diverse destinations. Core and Shackleford Banks lie within the Cape Lookout National Seashore, a wild maritime environment populated by plenty of wild ponies but not a single human. On the other hand, the towns of Bogue Banks—Atlantic Beach, Salter Path, Pine Knoll Shores, Indian Beach, and Emerald Isle—are classic beach towns, with clusters of motels and restaurants, and even a few towel shops and miniature golf courses. Both areas are great fun, though, Cape Lookout especially so for eco-tourists and history buffs, and Bogue Banks for those looking for a day on the beach followed by an evening chowing down on good fried seafood.

◖ CAPE LOOKOUT NATIONAL SEASHORE

Cape Lookout National Seashore (Headquarters 131 Charles St., Harkers Island, 252/728-2250, www.nps.gov/calo) is an otherworldly place, 56 miles of beach on four barrier islands, a long tape of sand so seemingly vulnerable to nature that it's hard to believe there were once several busy towns on its banks. Settled in the early 1700s, the towns of the south Core Banks made their living in fisheries that might seem brutal to today's seafood eaters—whaling, and catching dolphins and sea turtles, among the more mundane species. Portsmouth, at the north end of the park across the water from Ocracoke, was a busy port of great importance to the early economy of North Carolina. Portsmouth declined slowly, but catastrophe rained down all at once on the people of the southerly Shackleford Banks, who were driven out of their own long-established communities to start new lives on the mainland when a series of terrible hurricanes hit in the 1890s.

Islands often support unique ecosystems. Among the dunes, small patches of maritime forest fight for each drop of fresh water, while ghost forests of trees that were defeated by advancing saltwater look on resignedly. Along the endless beach, loggerhead turtles come ashore to lay their eggs, and in the waters just off the strand, three other species of sea turtles are sometimes seen. Wild horses roam the beaches and dunes and dolphins frequent both the ocean and sound sides of the islands. Other mammals, though, are all of the small and scrappy variety: raccoons, rodents, otters, and rabbits. Like all of coastal North Carolina, it's a great place for bird-watching, as it's located in a heavily traveled migratory flyway. (Pets are allowed, with leashes. The wild ponies on Shackleford Banks can pose a threat to dogs that get among them, and the dogs of course can frighten the horses, so be careful not to let them mingle should you and your dog find yourselves near the herd.)

Portsmouth Village

Portsmouth Village, at the northern tip of the Cape Lookout National Seashore, is a peaceful but eerie place. The village looks much as it did 100 years ago, the handsome houses and churches all tidy and in good repair, but with the exception of caretakers and summer volunteers, no one has lived here in nearly 40 years. In 1970, the last two residents moved away from what had once been a town of 700 people and one of the most important shipping ports in North Carolina. Founded before the Revolution, Portsmouth was a lightering station, a port where huge seagoing ships that had traveled across the ocean would stop, and have their cargo removed for transport across the shallow sounds in smaller boats. There is a visitors center located at Portsmouth, open varying hours April–October, where you can learn about the village before embarking on a stroll to explore the quiet streets.

In its busy history, Portsmouth was captured by the British during the War of 1812 and by the Yankees in the Civil War, underscoring its strategic importance. By the time of the Civil War, though, its utility as a way-station was already declining. An 1846 hurricane opened a new inlet at Hatteras, which quickly became a busy shipping channel. Then after abolition, the town's lightering trade was no longer profitable without slaves to perform much of the labor. The fishing and lifesaving businesses kept the town afloat for a couple

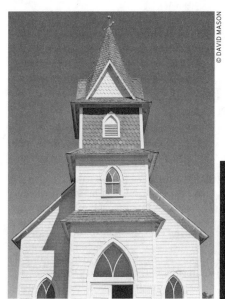

the church in Portsmouth Village

more generations, but Portsmouth was never the same.

Once a year, an amazing thing happens. Boatloads of people arrive on shore, and the church bell rings, and the sound of hymn singing comes through the open church doors. At the Portsmouth Homecoming, descendants of the people who lived here come from all over the state and country to pay tribute to their ancestral home. They have an old-time dinner on the grounds with much socializing and catching up, and then tour the little village together. It's like a family reunion, with the town itself the family's matriarch. On the other 364 days of the year, Portsmouth receives its share of tourists and Park Service caretakers, but one senses that it's already looking forward to the next spring, when its children will come home again.

Shackleford Banks

The once-busy villages of Diamond City and Shackleford Banks are like Portsmouth in that, though they have not been occupied for many years, the descendants of the people who lived here retain a profound attachment to their ancestors' homes. Diamond City and nearby communities met a spectacular end. The hurricane season of 1899 culminated in the San Ciriaco Hurricane, a disastrous storm that destroyed homes and forests, killed livestock, flooded gardens with saltwater, and washed the Shackleford dead out of their graves. The Bankers saw the writing on the wall, and moved to the mainland en masse, carrying as much of their property as would fit on boats. Some actually floated their houses across Core Sound. Harkers Island absorbed most of the refugee population (many also went to Morehead City), and their traditions are still an important part of Down East culture. Daily and weekly programs held at the Light Station Pavilion and the porch of the Keepers' Quarters during the summer months teach visitors about the natural and human history of Cape Lookout, including what day-to-day life was like for the keeper of the lighthouse and his family.

Descendants of the Bankers feel a deep spiritual bond to their ancestors' home, and for many years they would return frequently, occupying fish camps that they constructed along the beach. When the federal government bought the Banks, it was made known that the fish camps would soon be off-limits to their deedless owners. The outcry and bitterness that ensued testified to the depth of the Core Sounders' love of their ancestral grounds. The Park Service may have thought that the fish camps were of no more importance than duck blinds or tents—ephemeral and purely recreational structures. But to the fish camps' owners, the Banks was still home, even if they themselves had been born on the mainland and never lived there for longer than a fishing season—the camps were their homes every bit as much as their actual residences on the mainland. Retaining their pride of spiritual, if not legal, ownership, many burned down their own fish camps rather than allow the Park Service to destroy them.

Cape Lookout Lighthouse

By the time you arrive at the 1859 Cape Lookout Lighthouse (visitors center, 252/728-2250), you'll probably already have seen it portrayed

Shackleford Banks ponies

© NC DIVISION OF TOURISM

© BISSE BOWMAN

Cape Lookout Lighthouse, on the Cape Lookout National Seashore

on dozens of brochures, menus, business signs, and souvenirs. With its striking diamond pattern, it looks like a rattlesnake standing at attention. Because it is still a working lighthouse, visitors are allowed in on only four dates each year, 10 A.M.–3:30 P.M. Visit Cape Lookout National Seashore's website (www .nps.gov/calo) for open house dates and reservation information. The allotted times fill up almost immediately.

Accommodations

Morris Marina (877/956-5688, www.cape lookoutconcessions, $65–100) rents cabins at Great Island and Long Point. Cabins have hot and cold water, gas stoves, and furniture, but in some cases visitors must bring their own generators for lights, as well as linens and utensils. Rentals are not available from December through March. Book well in advance.

CAMPING

Camping is permitted within Cape Lookout National Seashore, though there are no designated campsites or camping amenities. Everything you bring must be carried back out when you leave. Campers can stay for up to 14 days.

Getting There

Except for the visitors center at Harkers Island, Cape Lookout National Seashore can only be reached by ferry. Portsmouth, at the northern end of the park, is a short ferry ride from Ocracoke, but Ocracoke is a very long ferry ride from Cedar Island. The **Cedar Island-Ocracoke Ferry** (800/856-0343) is part of the state ferry system, and costs $15 one-way for regular-sized vehicles (pets allowed). It takes 2.25 hours to cross Pamlico Sound, but the ride is fun, and embarking from Cedar Island feels like sailing off the edge of the earth. The **Ocracoke-Portsmouth ferry** is a passenger-only commercial route, licensed to Captain Rudy Austin. Call 252/928-4361 to ensure a seat. There's also a vehicle and passenger ferry, Morris Marina Kabin Kamps and Ferry Service (877/956-6568), **from Atlantic to Long Point** on the North Core Banks; leashed or in-vehicle pets are allowed. Most ferries operate between April and November, with some exceptions.

Commercial ferries cross every day **from mainland Carteret County** to the southern parts of the National Seashore. There is generally a ferry route between Davis and Great Island, but service can be variable; check the Cape Lookout National Seashore website (www.nps.gov/calo) for updates.

From Harkers Island, passenger ferries to Cape Lookout Lighthouse and Shackleford Banks include Calico Jacks (252/728-3575), Harkers Island Fishing Center (252/728-3907), Local Yokel (252/728-2759), and Island Ferry Adventures at Barbour's Marina (252/728-6181).

From Beaufort, passenger ferries include Outer Banks Ferry Service (252/728-4129), which goes to both Shackleford Banks and to Cape Lookout Lighthouse; Island Ferry Adventures (252/728-7555) and Mystery Tours (252/728-7827) run to Shackleford Banks. Morehead City's passenger-only

BEAUFORT

© RJONES0856

the ferry dock in Davis

Waterfront Ferry Service (252/726-7678) goes to Shackleford Banks as well. On-leash pets are generally allowed, but call ahead to confirm for Local Yokel, Island Ferry Adventures, and Waterfront Ferry Service.

BOGUE BANKS

The beaches of Bogue Banks are popular tourist spots, but they have a typically North Carolinian, laid-back feel, a quieter atmosphere than the fun-fun-fun neon jungles of other states' beaches. The major attractions here, Fort Macon State Park and the North Carolina Aquarium at Pine Knoll Shores, are a bit more cerebral than, say, amusement parks and bikini contests. In the surfing and boating, bars and restaurants, and the beach itself, there's also a bustle of activity to keep things hopping. Bogue, by the way, rhymes with "rogue."

◖ North Carolina Aquarium

The North Carolina Aquarium at Pine Knoll Shores (1 Roosevelt Blvd., Pine Knoll Shores, 866/294-3477, www.ncaquariums.com,

9 A.M.–5 P.M. daily, until 9 P.M. every Thurs. in July, $8 adults, $7 seniors, $6 children 17 and younger) is one of the state's three great coastal aquariums. Here at Pine Knoll Shores, exhibit highlights include: a 300,000-gallon aquarium in which sharks and other aquatic beasts go about their business in and around a replica German U-Boat (plenty of originals lie right off the coast and form homes for reef creatures); a "jellyfish gallery" (they really can be beautiful); a pair of river otters; and many other wonderful animals and habitats.

Trails from the parking lot lead into the maritime forests of the 568-acre **Theodore Roosevelt Natural Area** (1 Roosevelt Dr., Atlantic Beach, 252/726-3775).

Fort Macon State Park

At the eastern tip of Atlantic Beach is Fort Macon State Park (2300 E. Fort Macon Rd., 252/726-3775, www.ncsparks.net/foma.html, 9 A.M.–5:30 P.M. daily, fort open 8 A.M.–6 P.M. Oct.–Mar., 8 A.M.–7 P.M. Apr., May, and Sept., and 8 A.M.–8 P.M. June–Aug., bathhouse area

THE DECLINE OF THE FISHING INDUSTRY

It's ironic that along the coast of North Carolina, where for centuries fishing has been more than a business – it's been an entire culture – relatively little of the seafood served in restaurants or sold in markets nowadays is actually caught by local fishermen. Sitting in a dockside restaurant, looking out at fishermen unloading their day's haul, you may be eating shrimp that were flown in from Thailand, or fish from Chile, or oysters from France. Like the textile industry, North Carolina's commercial fisheries have suffered tremendously from global trade. There is, however, a growing concern for promoting the interests of local fisheries before it's too late – if it's not already. **Carteret Catch** is an organization dedicated to the promotion of the fishing industry here in Carteret County. At their website (www.carteretcatch.org), you can find out which local restaurants and fish markets are buying seafood from the fishermen who live and work in this community, rather than from international wholesalers.

As recently as 10 years ago, the shores and riverbanks of eastern North Carolina were covered with fish houses. Often small, family-run operations, fish houses were the best places in the world for seafood lovers, who could buy their favorite fish and shellfish as soon as the boats were unloaded. Today, things are very different. For reasons both environmental and economic, the old-time seafood house is nearly extinct. Declines in popular species of fish and shellfish have hit North Carolina's fishermen, like others around the world, painfully hard. Concurrently, the skyrocketing value of land along the coast – and up the rivers and along the back creeks and marshes – often renders such a business unsustainable. Owners of fish houses are either run out of business by the exponential rise of their property taxes, or give in to the temptation to sell their waterfront lots for more money than they might have made in years of fishing.

This book will help you find some of the last remaining fish houses and seafood restaurants that still serve catches right off the docks. Though they have become so few and far between, the effort in finding traditional seafood houses is certainly worthwhile. You'll taste some of the freshest, best seafood in the world, and you'll be helping give a critically threatened traditional way of life a fighting chance.

© BROOKE FULLER / 123RF.COM

shrimp boats near Swansboro

8 A.M.–5:30 P.M. Nov.–Feb., 8 A.M.–7 P.M. Mar.–Oct., 8 A.M.–8 P.M. Apr., May, and Sept., and 8 A.M.–9 P.M. June–Aug., bathhouse $4/day, $3 child). The central feature of the park is Fort Macon itself, an 1820s Federal fort that was a Confederate garrison for one year during the Civil War. Guided tours are offered, and there are exhibits inside the casemates. For such a stern, martial building, some of the interior spaces are surprisingly pretty.

Sports and Recreation

The ocean side of Bogue Banks offers plenty of public beach access. In each of the towns, from the northeast end of the island to the southwest end—Atlantic Beach, Pine Knoll Shores, Salter Path, Indian Beach, and Emerald Isle—there are parking lots, both municipal and private, free and for-fee.

Aside from the fort itself, the other big attraction at **Fort Macon** is the beach, which is bounded by the ocean, Bogue Sound, and Beaufort Inlet. Because there's a Coast Guard station on the Sound side, and a jetty along the Inlet, swimming is permitted only along one stretch of the ocean beach. A concession stand and bathhouse are located at the swimming beach.

Atlantic Beach Surf Shop (515 W. Fort Macon Rd., Atlantic Beach, 252/646-4944, www.absurfshop.com) gives individual ($50/hour) and group ($40/hour) surfing lessons on the beach at Pine Knoll Shores. Lessons are in the morning and early afternoon. Call for reservations.

Accommodations

The **Atlantis Lodge** (123 Salter Path Rd., Atlantic Beach, 800/682-7057, www.atlantislodge.com, $70–220) is an old, established, family-run motel. It has simple and reasonably priced efficiencies in a great beachfront location. Well-behaved pets are welcome for a per-pet-per-night fee. The **Clamdigger** (511 Salter Path Rd., Atlantic Beach, 800/338-1533, www.clamdiggerramadainn.com, $40–260) is another reliable choice, with all oceanfront rooms. Pets are not allowed. The **Windjammer** (103 Salter Path Rd., Atlantic Beach, 800/233-

6466, www.windjammerinn.com, $50–200) is another simple, comfortable motel, with decent rates through the high season.

Food

The **Channel Marker** (718 Atlantic Beach Causeway, Atlantic Beach, 252/247-2344) is an haute-er alternative to some of the old-timey fried seafood joints on Bogue Banks (which are also great—read on). Try the crab cakes with mango chutney, or the Greek shrimp salad. The extensive wine list stars wines from the opposite side of North Carolina, from the Biltmore Estate in Asheville.

White Swan Bar-B-Q and Chicken (2500-A W. Fort Macon Rd., Atlantic Beach, 252/726-9607) has been serving the Carolina trinity of barbecue, coleslaw, and hush puppies since 1960. They also flip a mean egg for breakfast.

The C **Big Oak Drive-In and Bar-B-Q** (1167 Salter Path Rd., 252/247-2588, www.bigoakdrivein.com) is a classic beach drive-in, a little red-white-and-blue-striped building with a walk-up counter and drive-up spaces. They're best known for their shrimpburgers ($4.95 large), a fried affair slathered with Big Oak's signature red sauce, coleslaw, and tartar sauce. Then there are the scallopburgers, oysterburgers, clamburgers, hamburgers, and barbecue, all cheap, and made for snacking on the beach.

Frost Seafood House (1300 Salter Path Rd., Salter Path, 252/247-3202) began in 1954 as a gas station and quickly became the restaurant that it is today. The Frost family catches its own shrimp and buys much of its other seafood locally. Be sure to request a taste of the "ching-a-ling sauce." Yet another community institution is the **Crab Shack** (140 Shore Dr., Salter Path, 252/247-3444). You'll find it behind the Methodist church in Salter Path. Operated by the Guthries (a family name that dates back to the dawn of time in this area, long before anyone thought of calling their home the "Crystal Coast"), the restaurant was wiped out in 2005 by Hurricane Ophelia, but they have since rebuilt, rolled up their sleeves, and plunged their hands back into the cornmeal.

WILMINGTON AND THE CAPE FEAR REGION

The Cape Fear region was and is very much a part of the Caribbean-basin culture that stretches up through the south Atlantic coast of North America—a world that reflects English, Spanish, and French adaptation to the tropics and, above all, to the profoundly transformative influence of the African cultures brought to the New World by captive slaves. Wilmington is part of the sorority that includes Havana, Caracas, Port au Prince, Santo Domingo, New Orleans, Savannah, and Charleston. Savannah, Charleston, and Wilmington are the main points of the Carolina Lowcountry, and like its closest sisters, Wilmington and the surrounding Cape Fear coast exhibits the richness of Afro-Caribbean culture in its architecture, cuisine, folklore, and speech.

Robeson County, along the South Carolina state line, is the geographic home of the Lumbee tribe, who are historically and spiritually tied to the beautiful blackwater Lumber River. The Lumbees are the largest tribe east of the Mississippi, yet many Americans have never heard of them. This is due in part to the fact that the government denies them federal recognition, a complex and highly contentious issue that casts a long shadow over much of the politics, economics, and history of this part of the state. A "non-reserved" tribe, the Lumbees have for centuries lived much as their white and African American neighbors have—a mostly rural existence, anchored in a profound devotion to the Christian faith. Their history is fascinating and often surprising, and can be explored by the traveler in and around the town of Pembroke.

HIGHLIGHTS

◖ **Wilmington's Historic District:** Wilmington's downtown reflects its glory days of commerce and high society. This is North Carolina's largest 19th-century historic district, a gorgeous collection of antebellum and late Victorian townhouses and commercial buildings, including many beautiful Southern iterations of the Italianate craze that preceded the Civil War (page 78).

◖ **Wrightsville Beach:** North Carolina has many wonderful beaches, but few can compare with Wrightsville for its pretty strand, easy public access, clear waters, and overall beauty (page 80).

◖ **Hammocks Beach State Park:** Accessible only by boat, one of the wildest and least disturbed Atlantic coast beaches, Bear Island is a popular stopover for migrating waterfowl and turtles (page 92).

◖ **Orton Plantation:** Orton's formal gardens embody the aesthetic of "Southern Gothic," juxtaposing the romantic idyll of the Old South with the mournful spookiness of moss-draped swamps, honking alligators, and the plantation's often tragic history. It's picturesque in the extreme (page 98).

◖ **Strike at the Wind:** One of North Carolina's premier outdoor dramas tells the story of the Henry Berry Lowrie gang, Reconstruction-era outlaws and heroes of Lumbee history. For 30 years, the play has been acted every summer by members of the tribe (page 103).

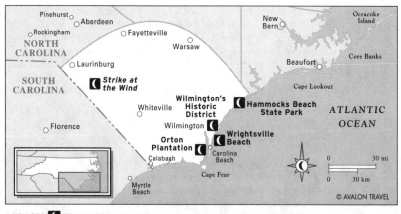

LOOK FOR ◖ TO FIND RECOMMENDED SIGHTS, ACTIVITIES, DINING, AND LODGING.

The area between Wilmington and Lumberton in the state's southeast corner is a strange, exotic waterscape (more so than a landscape) of seductively eerie swamps and backwaters. People from the Piedmont will turn up their noses at the swamps, claiming that they reek like rotten eggs and that the farmland's no good. But to those of us who are native to this corner of the Carolinas, our cypress knees and tannic creeks and nests of snakes and alligators make this a region of sinister but incomparable beauty—and swamp air is the best aromatherapy there is. In this little band of coastal counties straddling the state line, within a 100-mile radius of Wilmington, we share the native habitat—the only one in the world—of the Venus flytrap, a ferocious little plant of rather ghastly beauty. It somehow seems like an appropriate mascot for these weird backwaters.

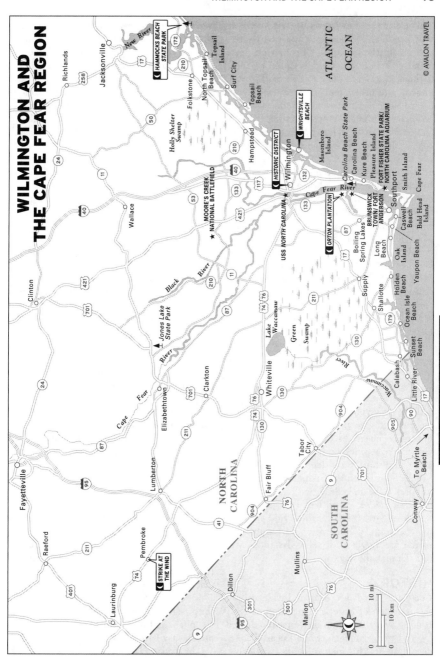

WILMINGTON AND THE CAPE FEAR REGION

© AVALON TRAVEL

ATLANTIC OCEAN

The greatest draw to this region, even more than colonial cobblestones and carnivorous plants, are the beaches of Brunswick, New Hanover, Pender, and Onslow Counties. Some of them, like Wrightsville and Topsail, are well known, and others remain comparatively secluded barrier island strands. In some ways the "Brunswick Islands," as visitors bureaus designate them, can be thought of as the northern edge of the famous Grand Strand area around Myrtle Beach, South Carolina. No square mile of this region could be mistaken for Myrtle Beach, though; even the beaches that are most liberally peppered with towel shops and miniature golf courses will seem positively bucolic in comparison. But those with an appreciation for Myrtle Beach's inimitable style, our own chaotically commercial, in-your-face Paris of the Pee Dee (one of the rivers that flows through the border region of the Carolinas), will be glad to know that it's only a few short miles away.

PLANNING YOUR TIME

Depending on which part of the Cape Fear area you're planning to explore, you have a range of good choices for your home base. Wilmington is an easy drive from pretty much anywhere in this region, giving ready access to the beaches to the north and south. It's so full of sights and activities that you'll probably want to stay here anyway and give yourself a day or more just to explore the city itself. If you're planning on visiting the beaches south of Wilmington, you might also want to consider staying in Myrtle Beach, South Carolina, which is about a 20 minutes' drive on U.S. 17 (with no traffic—in high season it's a very different story) from the state line. Farther inland, you'll find plenty of motels around Fayetteville and Lumberton, which are also a reasonable distance from Raleigh to make day trips.

HISTORY

The Cape Fear River, deep and wide, caught the attention of European explorers as early as 1524, when Giovanni de Verrazano drifted by, and two years later, when Lucas Vásquez de Ayllón and his men (including, possibly,

the first African slaves within the present-day United States) had a walk-about before proceeding to their appointment for shipwreck near Winyah Bay in South Carolina. Almost a century and a half later, William Hilton and explorers from the Massachusetts Bay Colony had a look for themselves. They were either disgusted with what they saw or knew they'd found a really good thing and wanted to psych out anyone with thoughts of a rival claim, because they left right away, and on their way out posted a sign at the tip of the Cape to the effect of, "Don't bother, the land's no good."

The next summer, John Vassall and a group of fellow Barbadians attempted settlement, but within a few years they abandoned the area. It wasn't until 1726, when Maurice Moore made the banks of the river his own on behalf of a group of allied families holding a patent to the area, that European settlement took. Moore lay out Brunswick Town, and his brother Roger established his own personal domain at Orton. (Today, only the ballast-stone foundations of houses and walls of the Anglican church remain at Brunswick, but Roger's home at Orton still stands.) The machinations of the Moore brothers led to the demise, or at least disintegration, of the Cape Fear tribe, who had been clinging to their land with varying success since the first Europeans arrived. Maurice Moore, with the aid of Tuscaroras, drove away many of the tribe, and then the few who remained at a settlement within present-day Carolina Beach State Park were slaughtered by Roger Moore in 1725. He claimed, whether truthfully or not, that a band of Cape Fear had attacked Orton.

Brunswick was briefly an important port, but it was soon eclipsed by Wilmington, a new settlement up the river established by an upstart group of non-Moores. By the time of the Revolution, it was Wilmington that dominated trade along the river. Meanwhile, a large population of Scottish immigrants had since the 1730s been farming and making a living from the pine forests (manufacturing naval stores—tar, pitch, and turpentine) in the area around present-day Fayetteville.

The Lower Cape Fear region, particularly

present-day Brunswick, New Hanover, Duplin, Bladen, and Onslow Counties, had a significantly larger slave population than most parts of North Carolina. The naval stores industry demanded a large workforce, and the plantations south of the river were to a large extent a continuation of the South Carolina Lowcountry economy, growing rice and indigo, crops that also led to the amassing of large populations of human chattel. All along the South Carolina and Georgia coasts, and into parts of Florida, these large communities of African-born and first-generation African American people established the culture now known as Gullah. Today the Gullah language and other aspects of the cultural heritage are most prominent around Charleston and on the islands just off the coast, and to a lesser extent in Savannah and points south, where a handful of communities still speak the Gullah language, a patois of English mixed with recognizably African vocabulary and grammar. The Gullah (sometimes called Geechee) accent, which has a heavy Caribbean resonance, can still be heard around Wilmington and the Brunswick Coast, in people who have never spoken any language but standard English. Aspects of Gullah traditions in cooking (gumbo, goobers/peanuts, okra), folklore (houses with steps, shutters, window panes, and roof-lines painted bright blue to keep bad luck away), and folk medicine (root doctoring) are still in evidence throughout the Lowcountry.

Another major cultural group in the Cape Fear region is that of the Lumbee tribe. They've been variously called the Croatan Indians, Pembroke Indians, and Indians of Robeson County. In the days of slavery they were identified as Free People of Color, and the ever-evolving laws of the state concerning their civil rights long denied them the rights to vote or bear arms.

The Lumbee also have a long history of resistance, and to the protection of their own land and rights. Most famously, the Lowry/Lowrie Band, outlaw heroes of the 19th century, defined the Lumbee cause for future generations. Another transformative moment in Lumbee history was the 1958 armed conflict near Maxton. Ku Klux Klan Grand Wizard "Catfish" Cole and about 40 other armed Klansmen held a rally here, at Hayes Pond. Local Lumbee, fed up with a recent wave of especially vicious intimidation at the hands of the Klan, showed up at the rally en masse—1,500 of them, all armed. The Lumbee shot out the one electric light and opened fire on the rally, causing the Klansmen to run like hell. The battle (which was won, incredibly, without a single death) was reported around the country, an energizing story for the cause of Native American rights, and a humiliation for the Ku Klux Klan.

In the late 20th and early 21st century, southeastern North Carolina's most prominent role is probably a military one. Fort Bragg, located in Fayetteville, is one of the country's largest Army installations, and the home base of thousands of the soldiers stationed in Iraq and Afghanistan. Nearby Pope Air Force Base is the home of the 43rd Airlift Wing, and at Jacksonville, the U.S. Marine Corps' II Expeditionary Force, among other major divisions, are stationed at Camp Lejeune. Numerous museums in Fayetteville and Jacksonville tell the world-changing history of the military men and women of southeastern North Carolina.

INFORMATION AND SERVICES

The several area hospitals include: two in Wilmington, **Cape Fear Hospital** (5301 Wrightsville Ave., 910/452-8100, www.nhhn.org) and the **New Hanover Regional Medical Center** (2132 S. 17th St., 910/343-7000, www.nhhn.org); two in Brunswick County, **Brunswick Community Hospital** in Supply (1 Medical Center Dr., 910/755-8121, www.brunswickcommunityhospital.com) and **Dosher Memorial Hospital** in Southport (924 N. Howe St., 910/457-3800, www.dosher.org); two more in Onslow County, **Onslow Memorial Hospital** in Jacksonville (317 Western Blvd., 910/577-2345, www.onslowmemorial.org) and the **Naval Hospital** at **Camp Lejeune** (100 Brewster Blvd., 910/451-1113, ej-www.med.navy.mil); and Fayetteville's **Cape Fear Valley Medical System** (1638 Owen Dr., 910/609-4000, www.capefear valley.com). Myrtle Beach's **Grand Strand Regional Medical Center** (809 82nd Pkwy., 843/692-1000, www.grandstrandmed.com) is not too far from the southernmost Brunswick communities. In an emergency, of course, calling 911 is the safest bet.

Extensive tourism and travel information is available from local convention and visitors bureaus: the **Wilmington/Cape Fear Coast CVB** (23 N. 3rd St., Wilmington, 877/406-2356, www.cape-fear.nc.us, 8:30 A.M.–5 P.M. Mon.–Fri., 9 A.M.–4 P.M. Sat., and 1–4 P.M. Sun.), and the **Brunswick County Chamber of Commerce** in Shallotte (4948 Main St., 800/426-6644, www.brunswickcounty chamber.org, 8:30 A.M.–5 P.M. Mon.–Fri.).

Wilmington

In many cities, economic slumps have an unexpected benefit: historic preservation. With Wilmington's growth at a standstill in much of the 20th century, there was no need to replace the old buildings and neighborhoods. As a result, downtown Wilmington has remained a vast museum of beautiful architecture from its early days, and that historic appeal accounts for much of its popularity today as a tourist destination.

The city is once again ascendant, an ever more desirable place to live as well as to vacation. Hollywood noticed the little city a couple of decades ago, and Wilmington has become one of the largest film and TV production sites east of Los Angeles. *Dawson's Creek, Matlock,* and *One Tree Hill* are just some of the well-known series filmed here, and noteworthy movies filmed at least partly in Wilmington include *Forrest Gump, Sleeping with the Enemy, I Know What You Did Last Summer,* and many more (though not, ironically, either version of *Cape Fear*). It's not unlikely that, strolling through city, you'll happen on a film crew at work.

HISTORY

Incorporated in 1739, Wilmington was strategically situated for maritime commerce. Its deep-water port made it a bustling shipping center for the export of lumber, rice, and naval stores (turpentine and tar tapped from the now nearly vanished longleaf pine forests). Businessmen came to Wilmington from around the world,

especially from Barbados, Scotland and northern Europe, and from the American colonies to the north. A fair number of New Englanders settled here, Nantucketers and other seafaring Yankees. In 1840, Wilmington became the eastern terminus of the 161-mile Wilmington and Weldon Railroad, which was at that time the longest railroad in the world. Now linking the commerce of land and sea with unprecedented efficiency, Wilmington's population exploded to almost 10,000 by 1860, making it the largest city in North Carolina.

During the War Between the States, the Wilmington and Weldon line was one of the crucial Confederate arteries for trade and transport, and Wilmington's port was a swarming hive of blockade runners. Its fall to the Union at the late date of January 1865 was a severe blow to the sinking Confederacy. Commerce allowed the city to weather the Civil War and Reconstruction, and it continued to grow and flourish. By 1890, the population had grown to 20,000. This was not an easy era socially, though, and tensions between white and black and Democrat and Republican Wilmingtonians exploded in the 1898 Wilmington Race Riot, one of the uglier incidents in the state's history. During the riot, a mob of white Democrats overthrew the city's Republican government, destroyed the black newspaper, the *Daily Record,* and murdered at least 22 African American citizens, leading to a radically accelerated revocation of the civil

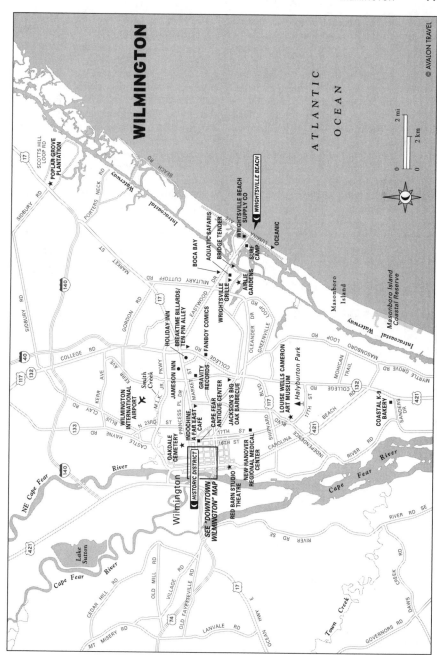

WILMINGTON

ATLANTIC OCEAN

© AVALON TRAVEL

WILMINGTON AND CAPE FEAR

SCOTTS HILL LOOP RD

★ POPLAR GROVE PLANTATION

17

SIDBURY RD

PORTERS NECK RD

Intracoastal Waterway

BEACH RD

WRIGHTSVILLE BEACH

WRIGHTSVILLE BEACH SUPPLY CO

BOCA BAY
AQUATIC SAFARIS
BRIDGE TENDER

SURF CAMP

OCEANIC

MILITARY CUTOFF RD

EASTWOOD RD

AIRLIE GARDENS

WRIGHTSVILLE GRILLE

MARKET ST

140

17

SIDBURY RD

GORDON RD

COLLEGE RD

40   117   132

HOLIDAY INN

BREAKTIME BILLARDS/
TEN PIN PIN ALLEY

FANBOY COMICS

COLLEGE RD

OLEANDER DR

GREENVILLE LOOP RD

MASONBORO LOOP RD

Masonboro Island Coastal Reserve

Intracoastal Waterway

MYRTLE GROVE RD

Smith Creek

WILMINGTON INTERNATIONAL AIRPORT

KERR AVE

M.L.K. JR. PKWY

CLAY RD

BLUE CLAY RD

133

CASTLE HAYNE RD

JAMESON INN

GRAVITY RECORDS

MARKET ST

INDOCHINE/
A FAR EAST CAFÉ

CAPE FEAR ANTIQUE CENTER

JACKSON'S BIG OAK BARBECUE

PRINCESS PL DR

N 23RD ST

17TH ST
16TH ST

LOUISE WELLS CAMERON ART MUSEUM

Halyburton Park

MOHICAN TRAIL

COLLEGE RD   132

421

17TH ST

BEACH RD

SHIPYARD BLVD

CAROLINA BEACH RD

COASTAL K-9 BAKERY

SANDERS DR

421

OAKDALE CEMETERY ★

HISTORIC DISTRICT

SEE "DOWNTOWN WILMINGTON" MAP

★ RED BARN STUDIO THEATRE

NEW HANOVER REGIONAL MEDICAL CENTER

INDEPENDENCE BLVD

Wilmington

140

NE Cape Fear River

421

Lake Sutton

Cape Fear River

Cape Fear River

RIVER RD

RIVER RD SE

CREEK RD

CEDAR HILL RD   OLD MILL RD   VILLAGE RD   OLD FAYETTEVILLE RD

74

MT MISERY RD   LANVALE RD   OCEAN HWY   17

GOVERNORS RD   DAWS RD

Town Creek

0   2 mi
0   2 km

rights gained by African Americans in North Carolina during Reconstruction.

In the early 20th century, North Carolina's economic pulse was increasingly to be found in the Piedmont, with its textile and manufacturing boom. In 1910, Charlotte surpassed Wilmington in population. Economically, the darkest hour came in 1960, with the relocation of the Atlantic Coast Line headquarters to Florida. The old port city experienced a slow decline in vitality throughout the 20th century. Today Wilmington is a city of about 100,000 people, with ever-increasing cachet and economic vitality as a retirement and vacation destination.

SIGHTS
◖ Historic District

Wilmington is to 19th-century architecture what Asheville is to that of the early 20th century. Having been the state's most populous city until around 1910, when Charlotte and its Piedmont neighbors left the old port city in their wake, Wilmington's downtown reflects its glory days of commerce and high society. This is North Carolina's largest 19th-century historic district, a gorgeous collection of antebellum and late Victorian townhouses and commercial buildings, including many beautiful Southern iterations of the Italianate craze that preceded the Civil War.

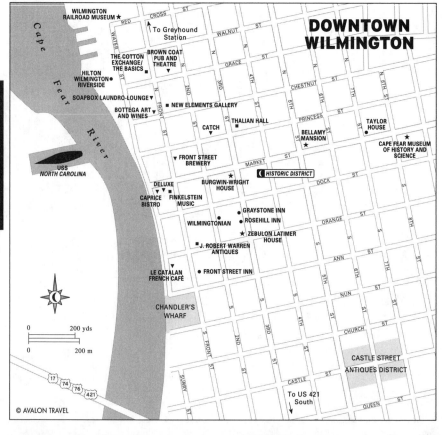

WILMINGTON AND CAPE FEAR

© AVALON TRAVEL

The Italianate Bellamy Mansion on Market Street is Wilmington's grandest antebellum house.

The **Bellamy Mansion** (503 Market St., 910/251-3700, www.bellamymansion.org, hourly tours 10 A.M.–5 P.M. Tues.–Sat., 1–5 P.M. Sun., $10 adults, $4 children under 12) is a spectacular example of Wilmington's late-antebellum Italianate mansions. This enormous white porticoed house ranks among the loveliest Southern city houses of its era. Built by planter Dr. John Bellamy just before the outbreak of the Civil War, the house was commandeered by the Yankees after the fall of Fort Fisher, and a trip to Washington and a pardon granted personally by President Andrew Johnson, a fellow North Carolinian, were required before Dr. Bellamy could pry his home out of Federal hands. In addition to the mansion, another highly significant building stands on the property: the slave quarters. This confined but rather handsome two-story brick building is one of the few surviving examples in this country of urban slave dwellings. Extensive renovations are underway to restore the quarters to its early appearance.

On the grounds of the Bellamy Mansion is a rare surviving example of urban slave quarters.

© SARAH BRYAN

The 1770 Burgwin-Wright House was built on top of a city jail.

The **Burgwin-Wright House** (224 Market St., 910/762-0570, www.burgwinwright house.com, tours 10 A.M.–3:30 P.M. Tues.– Sat., closed in January, $6 adults, $3 children under 12) has an oddly similar history to that of the Bellamy Mansion, despite being nearly a century older. John Burgwin (the emphasis is on the second syllable), a planter and the treasurer of the North Carolina colony, built the house in 1770 on top of the city's early jail. Soon thereafter, Wilmington became a theater of war, and the enemy, as was so often the case, took over the finest dwelling in town as its headquarters. In this case the occupier, who had a particularly fine eye for rebel digs, was Lord Cornwallis, then on the last leg of his campaign before falling into George Washington's trap. The Burgwin-Wright House is, like the Bellamy Mansion, a vision of white-columned porticoes shaded by ancient magnolias, but the architectural style here is a less ostentatious, though no less beautiful, 18th-century form, the mark of the wealthy merchant and planter class in the colonial

South Atlantic/Caribbean world. Seven terraced sections of garden surround the house; they are filled with native plants and many original landscape features, and make an intoxicating setting for an early spring stroll.

Yet another beautiful home in the historic district is the **Zebulon Latimer House** (126 S. Third St., 910/762-0492, www.latimerhouse .org, 10 A.M.–4 P.M. Mon.–Fri., noon–5 P.M. Sat., $8 adults, $4 if touring with a docent). The Latimer House is several years older than the Bellamy Mansion, but in its day was a little more fashion-forward, architecturally speaking. Mr. Latimer, a merchant from Connecticut, preferred a more urban expression of the Italianate style, a blocky, flat-roofed design with cast-iron cornices and other details that hint at the coming decades of Victorian aesthetics. Also located on the grounds is a very interesting two-story brick slave dwelling. The Latimer House is the headquarters of the Lower Cape Fear Historical Society, whose archive of regional history is important to genealogists and historic preservationists.

If you'd like to visit the Bellamy Mansion, Latimer House, and Burgwin-Wright House, be sure to buy a **three-house ticket** at the first house you visit. At $21, it will save you several bucks over what you'd pay were you to buy a ticket at each stop.

Wrightsville Beach

Wrightsville Beach, just outside of Wilmington, is easily one of the nicest beaches in the coastal Carolinas, which is a linear kingdom of beautiful strands. The beach is wide and easily accessible, visitor- and family-friendly, and simply beautiful. The water at Wrightsville often seems to be a brighter blue than one is accustomed to seeing this far north on the Atlantic coast, lending the feeling of a tropical coast. Wrightsville enjoys warm summertime water temperatures, a very large strand, and lots of lodging and rental choices along the beach. Numerous public beach access points (searchable at www.townofwrightsvillebeach.com/ accesspoints.htm), some wheelchair-accessible and some with showers and/or bathrooms, line

Lumina Avenue. The largest public parking lot, with 99 spaces, is at Beach Access #4, 2398 Lumina Avenue; #36 at 650 Lumina Avenue also has a large lot. They all fill up on busy days, but if you press on from one access point to the next, you'll eventually find a spot.

Historic Sights Around Wilmington
POPLAR GROVE PLANTATION

North of the city, about halfway between Wilmington and Topsail, is Poplar Grove Plantation (10200 U.S. 17 N., 910/686-9518, www.poplargrove.com, 9 A.M.–5 P.M. Mon.–Sat., noon–5 P.M. Sun, $8 adults, $7 seniors, $5 children ages 6–15). This antebellum peanut plantation features a beautiful 1850 big house, a restored tenant farmer's cabin, and other dependencies, as well as an extensive network of hiking trails through coastal forests and wetlands. In May, the plantation fills up with antique dealers and shoppers for the **Down Home Antique Fair.**

MOORE'S CREEK
NATIONAL BATTLEFIELD

Not surprisingly, given its importance as a maritime center, the environs of Wilmington have seen much military action over the last 300 years. About 20 miles northwest, outside the town of Currie near Burgaw, is the Moore's Creek National Battlefield (40 Patriots Hall Dr., Currie, 910/283-5591, www.nps.gov/mocr, 9 A.M.–5 P.M. daily except Thanksgiving, Christmas, and New Year's Day). The site commemorates the brief and bloody skirmish of February 1776 in which a Loyalist band of Scottish highlanders, kilted and piping, clashed with Patriot colonists. The revolutionaries fired on the Scotsmen with cannons as they crossed a bridge over Moore's Creek, which they'd previously booby-trapped, greasing it and removing planks. About 30 of the Crown's soldiers died, some drowning after they were blown off the bridge. Important as a moment in the American Revolution, this was also a noteworthy occasion in Scottish military history: it was the last major broadsword charge in Scottish history, led by the last Scottish clan army.

USS *NORTH CAROLINA*

Docked in the Cape Fear River, across from the Wilmington waterfront at Eagles Island,

© SARAH BRYAN

The USS *North Carolina* is docked in the Cape Fear River.

is the startling gray colossus of the battleship USS *North Carolina* (Eagles Island, 910/251-5797, www.battleshipnc.com, 8 A.M.–8 P.M. daily Memorial Day–Labor Day, 8 A.M.–5 P.M. daily Labor Day–Memorial Day, $9.50 adults, $5 ages 12 and under). This decommissioned World War II warship, which saw service at Guadalcanal, Iwo Jima, and many other important events in the Pacific theater, is a floating monument to the nearly 10,000 North Carolinians who died in WWII, and a museum of what life was like in a floating metal city.

Tours are self-guided, and include nine decks, the gun turrets and bridge, crew quarters, the sick deck, and the Roll of Honor display of the names of North Carolina's wartime dead. Allow yourself at least two hours to see it all. Visitors prone to claustrophobia might wish to stay above deck. The passageways and quarters below are close, dark, and very, very deep; from the heart of the ship it can take quite a while to get back out, and on a busy day the crowds can make the space seem even more constricted. (Just imagine how it would have felt to be in this ship in the middle of the Pacific, with nearly 2,000 other sailors aboard.)

The battleship is also one of North Carolina's most famous haunted houses, as it were—home to several ghosts who have been seen and heard on many occasions. The ship has been featured on the Sci-Fi Channel and on the ghost-hunting show *TAPS,* and is the subject of extensive writing and paranormal investigation. Visit www.hauntednc.com to hear some chilling unexplained voices caught on tape.

OAKDALE CEMETERY

In the mid-19th century, as Wilmington was bursting at the seams with new residents, the city's old cemeteries were becoming overcrowded with former residents. Oakdale Cemetery (520 N. 15th St., 910/762-5682, www.oakdalecemetery.org, 8 A.M.–5 P.M. daily year-round) was founded a ways from downtown to ease the subterranean traffic jam. It was designed in the park-like style of

graveyards that was popular at that time, and soon filled up with splendid funerary art—weeping angels, obelisks, willows—to set off the natural beauty of the place. (Oakdale's website has a primer of Victorian grave art symbolism.) Separate sections were reserved for Jewish burials and for victims of the 1862 yellow fever epidemic. It's a fascinating place for a quiet stroll.

Museums
CAPE FEAR MUSEUM OF HISTORY AND SCIENCE

The Cape Fear Museum of History and Science (814 Market St., 910/798-4370, www.capefearmuseum.com, 9 A.M.–5 P.M. Mon.–Sat., 1–5 P.M. Sun., closed Tues. Labor Day–Memorial Day, $6 adults, $5 students and seniors, $3 children 3–17) has exhibits about the ecology of the Cape Fear and its human history. Special treats are exhibits about giant native life forms, including the prehistoric ground sloth and Michael Jordan.

LOUISE WELLS CAMERON ART MUSEUM

The Louise Wells Cameron Art Museum (3201 S. 17th St., 910/395-5999, www.cameronartmuseum.com, 11 A.M.–5 P.M. Tues.–Thurs., Sat. and Sun., 11 A.M.–9 P.M. Fri., $8 adults, $5 students and members, $3 children 2–12) is one of the major art museums in North Carolina, a very modern gallery with a good permanent collection of art of many media, with a special emphasis on North Carolina artists. Masters represented include Mary Cassatt and Utagawa Hiroshige. Special exhibits change throughout the year.

WILMINGTON RAILROAD MUSEUM

The Wilmington Railroad Museum (505 Nutt St., 910/763-2634, www.wilmingtonrailroadmuseum.org, 10 A.M.–5 P.M. Mon.–Sat., 1–5 P.M. Sun. Apr. 1–Sept. 30, closed Sun. Oct.–Mar., $6 adults, $5 seniors and military, $3 ages 2–12) explores a crucial but now largely forgotten part of this city's history: its role as a railroad town. In 1840, Wilmington became the terminus for the world's longest continuous rail line, the Wilmington and Weldon. The Atlantic Coast Line Railroad (into which the W&W had merged around 1900) kept its headquarters at Wilmington until the 1960s, when it moved its offices, employees, and a devastatingly large portion of the city's economy, to Florida. All manner of railroad artifacts are on display in this great little museum, from timetables to locomotives. A classic iron horse, steam engine #250, sits on the track outside and has been restored beautifully.

Gardens and Parks
AIRLIE GARDENS
Airlie Gardens (300 Airlie Rd., 910/798-7700, www.airliegardens.org, 9 A.M.–5 P.M. Mon.–Sat. Jan. 2–Mar. 19, 9 A.M.–5 P.M. daily Mar. 20–Dec. 31, longer hours in Apr. and May, $5 adults, $3 children 6–12, no pets) is most famous for its countless azaleas, but this 100-year-old formal garden park has many remarkable features, including an oak tree believed to be nearly 500 years old, and the Minnie Evans Sculpture Garden and Bottle Chapel. Evans, a visionary African American artist whose mystical work is among the most prized of all "outsider art," was the gatekeeper here for 25 of her 95 years. Golf cart tours are available with 48 hours notice for visitors who are not mobile enough to walk the gardens. On second Saturdays, New Hanover County residents can get in free.

HALYBURTON PARK
A more natural landscape for hiking and biking is Halyburton Park (4099 S. 17th St., 910/341-7800, www.halyburtonpark.com, park open dawn–dusk daily, nature center 9 A.M.–5 P.M. Mon.–Sat.). The 58 acres of parkland, encircled by a 1.3-mile wheelchair-accessible trail and crisscrossed by interior trails, gives a beautiful glimpse of the environment of sandhills, Carolina bays (elliptical, often boggy depressions), and longleaf pine and oak forest that used to comprise so much of the natural landscape of this area.

illuminated live oak at Wilmington's Airlie Gardens

ANOLES OF CAROLINA

© PENNY WILLIAMS / 123RF.COM

During your visit to the Wilmington area, you'll almost certainly see anoles. These are the tiny green lizards that skitter up and down trees and along railings – impossibly fast, beady-eyed little emerald beasts. Sometimes called "chameleons" by the locals, anoles can change color to camouflage themselves against their backgrounds. They also like to puff out their crescent-shaped dewlaps, the little scarlet pouches under their chins, when they're courting, fighting, or otherwise advertising their importance.

Explorer John Lawson was quite taken with them, as he describes in his 1709 *A New Voyage to Carolina:*

> *Green lizards are very harmless and beautiful, having a little Bladder under their Throat, which they fill with Wind, and evacuate the same at Pleasure. They are of a most glorious Green, and very tame. They resort to the Walls of Houses in the Summer Season, and stand gazing on a Man, without any Concern or Fear. There are several other Colours of these Lizards, but none so beautiful as the green ones are.*

NEW HANOVER COUNTY ARBORETUM

The New Hanover County Arboretum (6206 Oleander Dr., 910/452-6393), also a popular walking spot, is a Cooperative Extension horticulture laboratory that showcases native plants and horticultural techniques in a varied five-acre garden setting.

ENTERTAINMENT AND EVENTS
Performing Arts

Thalian Hall (310 Chestnut St., 800/523-2820, www.thalianhall.com) was built in the mid-1850s and today is the last standing theater designed by the prominent architect John Montague Trimble. At the time of Thalian Hall's opening, fully one-tenth of the population of Wilmington could fit into the Thalian opera house, and the combination of the grand facility and Wilmington's longstanding love of the arts made this an important stop for many artists and productions touring the country in those days. It is still a major arts venue in the region, hosting performances of classical, jazz, bluegrass, and all sorts of other music, as well as ballet, children's theater, and more. Its resident theater company is the **Thalian Association** (910/251-1788, www.thalian.org), which traces its roots back to 1788 and has been named the official community theater company of North Carolina.

Also making its home at Thalian Hall is **Big Dawg Productions** (http://bigdawgproductions.org). They put on a variety of plays and musicals throughout the year, of all genres, and host the **New Play Festival,** a festival of first-time productions of work by authors under the age of 18. In the more than a dozen years of this festival, many works have premiered here that have gone on to much wider audiences and acclaim. Another Thalian company for nearly 25 years, the **Opera House Theatre Company** (910/762-4234, www.operahousetheatrecompany.net) has produced one varied season after another of big-name musicals and dramas, as well as the work of North Carolinian and Southern playwrights.

Thalian Hall was one of the most important venues in the region in the 19th century.

Rounding out the companies who perform at Thalian Hall is **Stageworks Youth Theater,** a community company of 10- to 17-year-old actors. Their productions "are not 'kiddie theater,'" as they write, "but substantial dramas, comedies, and musicals."

There's also a lot of theater going on outside the walls of Thalian Hall. One of the most critically acclaimed is **Red Barn Studio Theatre** (1122 South Third St., 910/762-0955, www .redbarnstudiotheatre.com). Actress Linda Lavin (of "Alice" fame) and her husband Steve Bakunas moved to Wilmington several years ago and converted an old garage into an intimate 50-seat theater. Red Barn's two to three annual productions are significant events in the cultural calendar of Eastern North Carolina.

Another popular local theater venue is the **Brown Coat Pub and Theatre** (111 Grace St., 910/341-0001, www.browncoattheatre.com),

home stage of the Guerilla Theatre Company. Brown Coat features all sorts of productions, from musical comedies to Shakespeare. It also hosts poetry nights, independent films, and a live weekly sitcom.

Festivals

Wilmington's best-known annual event is the **Azalea Festival** (910/794-4650, www.nc azaleafestival.org), which takes place in early April at venues throughout the city. It centers around the home and garden tours of Wilmington's most beautiful—and, at this time of year, azalea-festooned—historic sites. There is a dizzying slate of events, including a parade, circus, gospel concerts, shag and step competitions, even boxing matches. And like any self-respecting Southern town, it crowns royalty—in this case, the North Carolina Azalea Festival Queen, as well as its Princess, and the Queen's court, and a slate of cadets to escort all the Queen's ladies in waiting, and a phalanx of over 100 Azalea Belles. The Azalea Festival draws over 300,000 visitors, so book your accommodations well in advance; and if you're traveling through the area in early April but aren't coming to the festival, be forewarned, this will be one crowded town.

For all that Wilmington has become such a magnet for Hollywood, there's also a passion here for independent films. November's **Cucalorus Film Festival** (910/343-5995, www.cucalorus.org) has, over the course of a dozen years, become an important festival that draws viewers and filmmakers from around the world. Roughly 100 films are screened during each year's festival, which takes place at Thalian Hall and at the small Jengo's Playhouse (815 Princess St.) where the Cucalorus Foundation gives regular screenings throughout the year.

North of Wilmington, towards Topsail, the town of Hampstead has held its annual **North Carolina Spot Festival** (www.ncspotfestival .com) for nearly 50 years. The spot is a small fish that's a traditional favorite food on this coast, and in the fourth weekend of September hundreds of people gather here to deep-fry and

© CAPE FEAR CVB

Azalea Belles at Wilmington's annual Azalea Festival

gobble them up. There are bands and a pageant, but the fun centers around eating. It's a great little down-home festival.

Nightlife

The **Soapbox Laundro-Lounge** (255 N. Front St., 910/251-8500, www.soapboxlaundrolounge.com) has 11 washing machines, four dryers, and a good, long folding table. So what's it doing in the "Nightlife" section? It's also an important indie music venue (great bands, all kinds of music), a bar, a pool hall, and the setting of Monday-night Heavy Metal Bingo. ("No perfume scent down here, just the smell of PBR and ink.")

Bottega Art and Wines (208 N. Front St., 910/763-3737, www.bottegagallery.com) is an innovative, energetic gallery/venue/art space/wine bar. It's a gallery of contemporary art, to a large extent but not exclusively abstract, with frequently changing exhibitions. It's a serious wine bar, with a list a mile long of mainly American, Italian, and organic wines and beers, and a selection of nice hors d'oeuvres. It's also a venue for a rich slate of music performances and

poetry readings, and hosts arts gatherings like writers' forums and art discussion groups.

Breaktime Billiards/Ten Pin Alley (127 S. College Rd., 910/452-5455, www.breaktimetenpin.com, billiards and bowling 11 A.M.–2 A.M. daily, lounge 6 P.M.–2 A.M. Mon.–Fri., 11 A.M.–2 A.M. Sat. and Sun.) is a 30,000-square-foot entertainment palace. It consists of Breaktime Billiards, with 24 billiard tables and one regulation-size snooker table; Ten Pin Alley, with 24 bowling lanes and skee-ball; and in between them, the Lucky Strike Lounge, a full bar and snack shop with all manner of video games, and which hosts soft-tip dart and foosball tournaments. Put in an order for a meal and a beer or cocktail, and the staff will bring it to you if you're in the middle of a game.

Front Street Brewery (9 N. Front St., 910/251-1935, http://frontstreetbrewery.com, 11:30 A.M.–midnight Mon.–Wed., 11:30 A.M.–2 A.M. Thurs.–Sat., 11:30 A.M.–10 P.M. Sun., late-night menu starts at 10:30 P.M.) serves lunch and dinner, but what is most special is their menu of beers brewed on-site. They serve their own pilsner, IPA, and lager, Scottish and

Belgian ales, and their specialty River City Raspberry Wheat ale. The space has an attractive dark-paneled saloon decor, and plenty of seating areas to choose from, depending on whether you're looking for a sit-down meal or simply to gab over beer with friends.

SHOPPING
Shopping Centers

The buildings of **The Cotton Exchange** (Front and Grace Sts., 910/343-9896, www.shopcotton exchange.com) have housed all manner of businesses in over a century and a half of continuous occupation: a flour and hominy mill, a Chinese laundry, a peanut cleaning operation (really), a "mariner's saloon" (we'll say no more about that), and, of course, a cotton exchange. Today they're home to dozens of boutiques and restaurants, and lovely little specialty shops selling kites, beads, and spices. The author's favorites are **Occasions . . . Just Write** (O'Brien Building, 910/343.9033), a fine stationer's, and **Caravan Beads** (O'Brien Building, 910/343.0500), a pricey but intriguing bead shop.

Antiques and Consignment Stores

Along Castle Street, at the southern edge of the historic district, there is a growing district of antique shops, all within two to three blocks of each other. **Castle Keep Antiques** (507 Castle St., 910/343-6046) occupies an old church building, and has an absorbingly varied selection, with a more rural bent than the surrounding shops, many of which specialize in fine furniture. Also be sure to stop in at **New Castle Antiques Center** (606 Castle St., 910/341-7228), and **Maggy's Antiques** (511 Castle St., 910/343-5200).

In the riverfront area, **Antiques of Old Wilmington** (25 S. Front St., 910/763-5188) and **Silk Road Antiques** (103 S. Front St., 910/343-1718) are within an easy walk of many restaurants, and each other. An especially intriguing shop is **J. Robert Warren Antiques** (110 Orange St., 910/762-6077, www.jrobert warrenantiques.com), which occupies an 1810 townhouse downtown. Warren specializes in

fine and rare antiques from North Carolina, like furniture from the early masters, the work of colonial silversmiths, prints and paintings of early Carolinians and Carolina scenes, nautical hardware from old ships, and much more.

On Market Street headed away from downtown is **Cape Fear Antique Center** (1606 Market St., 910/763-1837, www.capefear antiquecenter.com), which carries fancy vintage home furnishings, from bedroom and dining room furniture to desks and armoires, in beautiful tones of wood, as well as a nice selection of antique jewelry.

Books and Comics

Wilmington has quite a few nice bookstores, both retail and used. **McAllister & Solomon** (4402-1 Wrightsville Ave., 910/350-0189, www.mcallisterandsolomon.com) stocks over 20,000 used and rare books, a great treat for collectors to explore. **Two Sisters Bookery** (318 Nutt St., Cotton Exchange, 910/762-4444, www.twosistersbookery.com, 10 A.M.–6 P.M. Mon.–Sat., noon–6 P.M. Sun.) is a nice little independent bookseller at the Cotton Exchange, with an inventory covering all genres and subject matters, and a calendar full of readings by favorite authors. Also excellent is **Pomegranate Books** (4418 Park Ave., 910/452-1107, www.pombooks.net, 10 A.M.–6 P.M. Mon.–Sat.), which has a progressive bent and a wide selection of good reads.

Fanboy Comics (3901-A Wrightsville Ave., 910/452-7828, www.fanboycomics.biz, 11 A.M.–9 P.M. Mon.–Wed., 11 A.M.–11 P.M. Thurs.–Sat., noon–9 P.M. Sun.) specializes in buying and selling Silver and Bronze Age superhero comics, a period beginning in the 1950s, and ending, at least in terms of Fanboy's stock, around 1977. The Silver and Bronze Ages have many defining characteristics, among which are graphic and technical innovations, the gradual transformation of two-dimensional superheroes into more fully developed characters with human problems and cares, and the introduction of science fiction and, eventually, '70s noir storylines. Fanboy carries an amazing stock, and they also host frequent gaming events and tournaments.

Galleries and Art Studios
New Elements Gallery (216 N. Front St., 910/343-8997, www.newelementsgallery.com, Tues.–Sat. 11 A.M.–5:30 P.M.) has been a leading institution in Wilmington's art scene since 1985. Featuring contemporary art in a wide variety of styles and media, New Elements has a special focus on artists from North Carolina and the wider Southeast.

An unusual retail art gallery is found between Wilmington and Wrightsville, the 23,000-square-foot **Racine Center for the Arts** (203 Racine Dr., 910/452-2073, www.galleryatracine.com). In addition to the sales gallery, it has art space for classes in pottery, stained glass, and other crafts, and operates the Firebird Paint Your Pottery and Art Studio. Visitors can show up at the Firebird without reservations, and go right to work on their own pottery and mosaics with the help of staff.

Music
Finkelstein Music (6 South Front St., 910/762-5662, www.finkelsteins.com) is a family business that has been at this site, a great old commercial building on a busy downtown corner, for over 100 years. It began as a dry good store, but gradually evolved into today's music store, which carries a great selection of guitars, electric basses, and percussion.

Gravity Records (125-1 S. Kerr Ave., 910/392-2414, www.gravity-records.com) is a record store with a wide selection of all sorts of music. They sell CDs and DVDs, but the focus is on LP records. They've got a huge stock of vinyl, and they also sell and service turntables. Another good choice is **Yellow Dog Discs** (341-12 S. College Rd., 910/792-0082, www.myspace.com/yellowdogdiscs), a buy/sell/trade store for CDs, DVDs, LPs, games, and posters. Their motto is "Skip free, guaranteed."

For Dogs
Coastal K-9 Bakery (5905 #9 Carolina Beach Rd., 866/794-4014, www.coastalk9bakery.com, 10 A.M.–6 P.M. Mon.–Sat., 1–5 P.M. Sun.) sells fresh-baked gourmet dog treats, including various organic and hypoallergenic goodies,

Carolina barbecue biscuits, liver brownies, and even vegetarian bacon bits.

SPORTS AND RECREATION
Masonboro Island
A half-hour's boat ride from Wrightsville Beach is Masonboro Island, an undeveloped barrier island that is a favorite spot for birding, shelling, and camping. The **Cape Fear Naturalist** (910/200-4002, www.capefearnaturalist.com) operates the Wrightsville Water Taxi, which docks across the street from the Blockade Runner Hotel (275 Waynick Blvd.), and offers daily shuttle service to the island in season. The boat leaves the dock at 9 A.M. Monday–Saturday, and returns at 3 P.M. Roundtrip costs $20 for adults, $10 for children under 12. Call ahead for reservations.

Surfing
Wrightsville Beach is a very popular destination for East Coast surfers and is home to several surfing schools. **Surf Camp** (530 Causeway Dr., 866/844-7873, www.wbsurfcamp.com) is probably the area's largest surfing instruction provider. They teach a staggering number of multi-day camps; one-day courses; kids-only, teenagers-only, women-only, and whole-family offerings; and classes in safety as well as technique. **Wrightsville Beach Supply Company** (1 N. Lumina Ave., 910/256-8821, www.wbsupplyco.com) has a retail store, and offers surf classes in the summertime (8–10 A.M. daily, $45 including board rental) and private lessons ($60) arranged according to the customer's schedule. **Crystal South Surf Camp** (Public access #39 on the beach, 910/395-4431, www.crystalsouthsurfcamp.com) is a family-run operation that gives group and individual five-day instruction for all ages.

Other Water Sports
Salt Marsh Kayaks (Shop 222 Old Causeway Dr., rental facility 275 Waynick Blvd., 866/655-2925, http://saltmarshkayakcompany.com), rents kayaks (sit-insides and sit-on-tops, singles and tandems) and sailboats, gives classes in sailing and kayaking, and guides tours through

some of the area's most interesting waterscapes. **Il Dolphins Sailing School** (222 Old Causeway Dr., 910/619-1646, www.iidolphins.com), which operates out of the Salt Marsh Kayaks storefront, teaches courses from Keelboat Sailing 101 to more advanced classes in navigation. They also run evening ocean cruises ($50 individuals, $95 couples, $45 children under 13) departing from the Blockade Runner docks.

Aquatic Safaris (6800-1A Wrightsville Ave., 910/392-4386, www.aquaticsafaris.com, in-season 9 A.M.–6 P.M. Mon.–Thurs., 9 A.M.–7 P.M. Fri., 6:30 A.M.–6 P.M. Sat., 6:30 A.M.–5 P.M. Sun., out of season 10 A.M.–6 P.M. Mon.–Fri., 10 A.M.–5 P.M. Sat., noon–4 P.M. Sun.) runs charter diving trips to shipwrecks (some sunken for artificial reefs, some scuttled during WWII when U-boats were a frequent sight here) and other underwater environments. They also teach dive classes and rent equipment.

Spectator Sports

Wilmington has its own professional basketball team, in the Continental Basketball League. The **Wilmington Sea Dawgs** (910/791-6523, www.goseadawgs.com, adults $8, children $5) play in the Schwartz Center at Cape Fear Community College, downtown at 601 N. Front Street. In baseball, the **Wilmington Sharks** (910/343-5621, www.wilmingtonsharks.com, box seats $8, general admission $5), a Coastal Plains League team, play at Legion Sports Complex at 2131 Carolina Beach Road.

ACCOMMODATIONS

Wilmington overflows with historic bed-and-breakfasts. **Front Street Inn** (215 S. Front St., 800/336-8184, www.frontstreetinn.com, $139–239) is a tiny boutique hotel in the historic district, one block from the Cape Fear River and easy walking distance from the restaurants and shops at Market and Front Streets. The Inn occupies the old Salvation Army of the Carolinas building, an attractive brick city building with arched windows and bright, airy rooms. For comfortable and classy lodging in the heart of the historic district, the Front Street Inn is a best bet.

The **Wilmingtonian** (101 S. Second St., 910/343-1800, www.thewilmingtonian.com, $87–325/night) is a complex of five buildings, four of which are renovated historic structures, from the 1841 de Rosset House to a 1950s convent. The de Rosset House is an utterly fabulous Italianate mansion, one of the most recognizable buildings in Wilmington. For $325 ($250 out of season), you can stay in the Cupola Suite, a spectacular aerie with a panoramic view of the port. The **Rosehill Inn** (114 S. Third St., 800/815-0250, www.rosehill.com, $90–200) occupies a pretty 1848 residence three blocks from the river. The flowery high-B&B-style decor suits the house well, making for elegant but comfy quarters. The **Taylor House** (14 N. Seventh St., 800/382-9982, www.taylorhousebb.com, $125–140) is an absolutely lovely 1905 home—rather subdued in design when compared to some of the architectural manifestos nearby, but in a very attractive way. The pretty, sunny rooms promise relaxation. The famous **Graystone Inn** (100 S. Third St., 888/763-4773, www.graystoneinn.com, $159–379) was built in the same year as the Taylor House, but its builder, the widow Elizabeth Bridgers, had a very different aesthetic. The splendor of the palace first known as the Bridger House reflects the fortune of Mrs. Bridgers' late husband, a former Confederate congressman and one of the most influential figures in Wilmington's days as a railroad center.

These are by no means the only excellent bed-and-breakfast inns in Wilmington; the city is full of them. Check in with the **Cape Fear Convention and Visitors Bureau** (www.cape-fear.nc.us) for a comprehensive listing.

Another plush place to stay in the downtown area is the **Hilton Wilmington Riverside** (301 N. Water St., 888/324-8170, www.wilmingtonhilton.com). Located right on the river, many of the rooms have a great view. The shops, restaurants, and galleries of the riverfront are right outside the front door, making this a great place to stay if you're planning to enjoy Wilmington's downtown.

More affordable options are plentiful,

especially on Market Street a couple of miles from downtown. Wilmington's **Holiday Inn** (5032 Market St., 866/553-0169, www.wilmingtonhi.com, $65–135) is clean and comfortable, and just a few minutes' drive from the historic district. Nearby is the **Jameson Inn** (5102 Dunlea Ct., 910/452-9828, www.jamesoninns.com, from $65), another fine choice. The Jameson Inn is a little hard to find, hidden behind other buildings. From Market Street, turn onto New Centre Drive, and look for the sign across the street from Target.

FOOD
Continental
Caprice Bistro (10 Market St., 910/815-0810, www.capricebistro.com, 5–10 P.M. Sun.–Thurs., 5 P.M.–midnight Fri. and Sat., bar open until 2 A.M.) entrées $13–22) is an absolutely wonderful little café and bar, hosted by Thierry and Patricia Moity. The French cuisine here is delicious, and the wine list is extensive. This is one of the best restaurants in town, and well worth a visit.

Le Catalan French Café (224 S. Water St., 910/815-0200, www.lecatalan.com, from 11:30 A.M. for lunch and dinner Tues.–Sat., and Sun. in the summer) couldn't have a nicer location, on the Riverwalk in the old downtown. They serve wonderful classic French food—quiches and *feuilletés*, beef bourguignonne on winter Fridays, and a chocolate mousse for which they are famous. Their greatest draw, though, is the wine list (and attached wine store). The proprietor, Pierre Penegre, is a Cordon Bleu–certified oenologist, and is frequently on hand to make recommendations.

Seafood
Wrightsville Beach's **Bridge Tender** (1414 Airlie Rd., Wilmington, 910/256-4519, www.thebridgetender.com, lunch 11:30 A.M.–2 P.M. daily, dinner from 5 P.M. daily, bar open all day, $20–35) has been in business for over 30 years and is an icon of the local restaurant scene. The atmosphere is simple and elegant, with a dockside view. Entrées focus on seafood and Angus beef, with an extensive à la carte menu from which

you can create delicious combinations of your favorite seafood and the Bridge Tender's special sauces. A sushi menu rounds out the appetizers, and a long wine list complements everything.

When you see a restaurant set in a really beautiful location, you dearly hope the food is as good as the view. Such is the case at Wrightsville's **Oceanic** (703 S. Lumina, Wrightsville Beach, 910/256-5551, www.oceanicrestaurant.com). The Wilmington *Star-News* has repeatedly voted it the Best Seafood Restaurant in Wilmington, and it receives similar word-of-mouth accolades right and left. It occupies a big old house right on the beach, with a wraparound porch and a pier. For an extra-special experience, ask for a table on the pier.

The relatively new **Wrightsville Grille** (6766 Wrightsville Ave., Suite J at Galleria Shopping Center, Wrightsville Beach, 910/509-9839, www.wrightsvillegrille.com) is roundly praised for its crab cakes ($20 for two), known for being super-hefty and having a high crab-to-breading ratio. The menu has a lot of casual café favorites, burgers and sandwiches, as well as extensive seafood and meat selections, and a daily "Chocoholic Special."

Southern and Barbecue
Right downtown at the Cotton Exchange, facing Front Street is **The Basics** (319 Front St., 910/343-1050, breakfast Mon.–Fri. 8 A.M.–11 A.M., lunch Mon.–Fri. 11 A.M.–4 P.M., dinner nightly at 5 P.M., Sat. and Sun. brunch 11 A.M.–4 P.M.). In a streamlined, simple setting, The Basics serves comfort food classics, Southern-style. Be sure to try the Coca-Cola cake, a surprisingly delicious Southern delicacy.

Also downtown, the **Dixie Grill** (116 Market St., 910/762-7280, www.dixiegrillwilmington.com, $6–15) is an old-fashioned diner that serves as a favorite local hangout. Southern diner food is the specialty here. The fried green tomato BLT is perfectly delicious.

In business since 1984, **€ Jackson's Big Oak Barbecue** (920 S. Kerr Ave., 910/799-1581, all dishes under $8), is an old favorite. Their motto is, "We ain't fancy, but we sure are good." Good old vinegary, Eastern North Carolina–style pork barbeque is the main item, though you can pick from Brunswick stew, fried chicken, and a mess of country vegetables. You'll get hush puppies and cornsticks at the table, but it will be worth your while not to fill up too fast—the cobblers and banana pudding are great.

Another star of Southern cooking is **Casey's Buffet Barbecue and Home Cookin'** (5559 Oleander Dr., 910/798-2913, lunch Tues.–Sat., dinner Wed.–Sun.). Here you can feast on barbecue and Brunswick stew, fried chicken and catfish, okra and collard greens. Adventurous Yankees might want to venture into the Southern culinary backwoods and try chitterlings (pronounced "chitlins," of course) and chicken gizzards. The folks at the next table are enjoying them, so why not you?

Eclectic American

Keith Rhodes, a Wilmington native and chef of **Deluxe** (114 Market St., 910/251-0333, www.deluxenc.com, $16–35) beat out 69 other top chefs to win first place in the Goodness Grows championship, a statewide title. The menu at Deluxe features stunning high-gourmet creations that pay homage to down-home Southern cooking, including confit of bobwhite quail on apple corn-cake and a bed of braised collards, buttermilk-fried crispy calamari, and white soy-molasses grilled lamb chops. Deluxe deserves additional gold stars for two special features: excellent vegetarian selections and menu descriptions that identify locally caught and grown ingredients.

Flaming Amy's Burrito Barn (4002 Oleander Dr., 910/799-2919, www.flaming amysburritobarn.com, 11 A.M.–10 P.M. daily) is, in their own words, "Hot, fast, cheap, and easy." They've got a long menu with 20 specialty burritos (Greek, Philly steak, Thai), eight fresh salsas, and bottled and on-tap beers. It's very inexpensive—you can eat well for under $10, drinks included. Frequent special promotions include Tattoo Tuesdays; if you show the cashier your tattoo (come on, we all know you've got one), you can take 10 percent off your meal.

Boca Bay (2025 Eastwood Rd., 910/256-1887, www.bocabayrestaurant.com, 5–10 P.M. Mon.–Thurs., 5–11 P.M. Fri. and Sat., brunch 9 A.M.–2 P.M. Sun., entrées $11–20) serves a tapas-style menu of sushi, stir fries, and heartier entrées, all very tasty. Vegetarian options are fairly limited, but you can cobble together a meal of tapas, salad, and sides.

Catch (215 Princess St., 910/762-2841, www .catchwilmingtonnc.com, lunch 11 A.M.–2 P.M. Mon.–Fri., dinner Wed.–Fri. 5:30–9 P.M., entrées $13–21) is a tiny and often crowded seafood restaurant that serves what Chef Keith Rhodes terms "Viet-Southern" cuisine. Chef Rhodes, who has twice won the Best Dish in North Carolina contest, uses locally caught seafood, ensuring the freshest ingredients possible.

Asian

Indochine, A Far East Café (7 Wayne Dr. at Market St., 910/251-9229, www.indo chinewilmington.com, lunch 11 A.M.–2 P.M. Tues.–Thurs., 11 A.M.–3 P.M. Sat., dinner 5–10 P.M. Mon.–Sun.) specializes in Thai and Vietnamese cuisine, and has an extensive vegetarian menu, and plenty of options for nonvegetarians as well. Though this restaurant is not downtown but a ways out Market Street, it's worth the drive. Try the vegetarian samosa egg rolls as an appetizer.

Double Happiness (4403 Wrightsville Ave., 910/313-1088, lunch and dinner) is a popular Chinese and Malaysian restaurant, known for serving traditional dishes that are a refreshing departure from the standard canon of American-Chinese restaurants. The setting is original too, without, as one local food critic wrote, "a buffet or glamour food photos over a hospital-white take-out counter." You can choose between regular booths and traditional floor seating. If you're lucky, you might be present when the chef decides to send around rice balls, a sweet dessert snack, for everyone on the house.

NORTH OF WILMINGTON
Topsail Island

In the manner of an old salt, Topsail is

pronounced "Tops'l." The three towns on Topsail Island—Topsail Beach, North Topsail Beach, and Surf City—are popular beach communities; they're less commercial than some of their counterparts elsewhere along the coast, but still destinations for throngs of visitors in the summer months. A swing bridge gives access to the island at Surf City (the bridge opens around the beginning of each hour, so expect backups) and a high bridge between Sneads Ferry and North Topsail.

Among Topsail's claims to fame is its importance in the conservation of sea turtle populations. The **Karen Beasley Sea Turtle Rescue and Rehabilitation Center** (822 Carolina Ave., Topsail Beach, www.seaturtlehospital .org, visiting hours 2–4 P.M. Mon., Tues., and Thurs.–Sat. in June, July, and Aug.) treats sea turtles that have been injured by sharks or boats, or are ill or stranded. Its 24 enormous tubs, which look something like the vats at a beer brewery, provide safe places for the animals to recover from their injuries and recoup their strength before being released back into the ocean. Guardian angels from the hospital also patrol the full shoreline of Topsail Island every morning in the summertime, before the crowds arrive, to identify and protect any new clutches of eggs that were laid overnight. Founder Jean Beasley has been featured as a Hero of the Year on the Animal Planet channel. Unlike most wildlife rehabilitation centers, this hospital allows the public to tour the facilities (during limited summer hours) and catch a glimpse of the patients.

Also at Topsail Beach is the **Missiles and More Museum** (720 Channel Ave., 910/328-8663, www.topsailmissilesmuseum.org). This little museum commemorates a rather peculiar chapter in the island's history: when it was used by the U.S. government for a project called Operation Bumblebee. During Operation Bumblebee, Topsail was a proving ground for missiles, and the work done here led to major advancements in missile technology and the development of a precursor of the ram jet engine used later in supersonic jet design. Exhibits include real warheads left over

from the tests, and even one that washed up on the beach 50 years after being fired out to sea. Especially interesting to lovers of projectiles will be the 1940s color film of missile firings here at Topsail.

Jacksonville

Jacksonville is best known as the home of **Camp Lejeune,** a massive Marine installation that dates to 1941. Lejeune is the home base of the II Marine Expeditionary Force, and of MARSOC, the Marine Corps division of U.S. Special Operations Command. The nearly 250 square miles that comprise the base include extensive beaches, where servicemen and women receive training in amphibious assault skills.

Construction has begun for the Museum of the Marine (www.mcmuseum.com), a major commemorative museum that will explore the history of this branch of the military, with particular focus on the contributions of Marines from and trained in North Carolina.

Camp Johnson, a satellite installation of Camp Lejeune, used to be known as Montford Point, and was the home of the famous African American Montford Point Marines. Their history, a crucial chapter in the integration of the United States Armed Forces, is paid tribute at the **Montford Point Marine Museum** (Building 101, East Wing, Camp Gilbert Johnson, 910/450-1340, www.montfordpoint marines.com, 11 A.M.–2 P.M. and 4–7 P.M., Tues. and Thurs., and 11 A.M.–4 P.M. Sat.).

◖ Hammocks Beach State Park

At the very appealing little fishing town of Swansboro you'll find the mainland side of Hammocks Beach State Park (1572 Hammocks Beach Rd., 910/326-4881, www.ncparks.gov/ Visit/parks/habe/main.php, 8 A.M.–6 P.M. daily Sept.–May, 8 A.M.–7 P.M. daily June–Aug.). Most of the park lies on the other side of a maze of marshes, on Bear and Huggins Islands. These wild, totally undeveloped islands are important havens for migratory waterfowl and nesting loggerhead sea turtles. Bear Island is three and a half miles long and less than a mile wide, surrounded by the Atlantic

Ocean, Intracoastal Waterway, Bogue and Bear Inlets, and wild salt marshes. Much of the island is covered by sandy beaches and dunes. A great place to swim, Bear Island has a bath house complex with a snack bar, restrooms, and outdoor showers. Huggins Island, by contrast, is significantly smaller, and covered in ecologically significant maritime forest and lowland marshes. Two paddle trails, one just over two and a half miles and the other six miles, weave through the marshes that surround the islands.

Camping is permitted on Bear Island, in reserved and first-come sites near the beach and inlet, with restrooms and showers available nearby.

A private boat or **passenger ferry** (910/326-4881, $5 adults, $3 seniors and children) are the only ways to reach the islands. The ferry's schedule varies by days of the week and season: Wednesday–Saturday May and September and Friday–Saturday April and October, departs from the mainland every half-hour 9:30 A.M.–4:30 P.M., departs from the island every hour 10 A.M.–5 P.M.; Monday–Tuesday Memorial Day–Labor Day departs from the mainland every hour 9:30 A.M.–5:30 P.M., departs from the island every hour 10 A.M.–6 P.M.; Wednesday–Sunday Memorial Day–Labor Day departs from the mainland every half-hour 9:30 A.M.–5:30 P.M., departs from the island every half-hour 10 A.M.–6 P.M.

GETTING THERE AND AROUND

Wilmington is the eastern terminus of I-40, more than 300 miles east of Asheville, approximately 120 miles east of Raleigh. The Cape Fear region is also crossed by a major north–south route, U.S. 17, the old Kings Highway of colonial times. Wilmington is roughly equidistant along U.S. 17 between Jacksonville to the north and Myrtle Beach, South Carolina, to the south; both cities are about an hour away. Wilmington International Airport serves the region with flights to and from East Coast cities. For a wider selection of routes, it may be worthwhile to consider flying into Myrtle Beach or Raleigh, and renting a car. If driving to Wilmington from the Myrtle Beach airport, add another half-hour or hour to get through Myrtle Beach traffic (particularly in the summer), as the airport there is on the southern edge of town. If driving from Raleigh-Durham International Airport, figure on the trip taking at least 2.5 hours. There is no passenger train service to Wilmington.

Wave Transit (910/343-0106, www.wave transit.com), Wilmington's public transportation system, operates buses throughout the metropolitan area and trolleys in the historic district. Fares are very low—$1 max, one-way. If you're planning on exploring outside the city, though, your best bet is to go by car.

The Southern Coast

From the beaches of Brunswick and New Hanover County to the swampy, subtropical fringes of land behind the dunes, this little corner of the state is incredibly special—and is one of the most beautiful parts of North Carolina.

There are a string of beaches here, starting with Carolina Beach and Kure, just south of Wilmington, and descending through the "Brunswick Islands," as they are designated in tourist literature. Most of these beaches are low-key, quiet family beaches, largely lined with

residential and rental properties. They're crowded in the summertime, of course, but are still much more laid back than Myrtle Beach, over the state line to the south, and even Wrightsville and some of the "Crystal Coast" beaches.

You'll see some distinctive wildlife here, too. The first you'll notice, more likely than not, is the ubiquitous green anole (called "chameleons" by many locals). These tiny lizards, normally a bright lime green, but able to fade to brown when invisibility is called for, are everywhere—skittering up porch columns and along balcony railings, peering at you around corners, hiding between the fronds of palmetto trees. The males put on a big show by puffing out their strawberry-colored dewlaps. Generations of Lowcountry children have spent thousands of frustrated hours trying to catch them, usually with next to no success. If you catch them from the front, they'll bite (albeit rather harmlessly), and if you catch them from behind, they'll be only too happy to cede to you their writhing tails, while the rest of them keeps running. But from a respectful distance, they're amusing companions all along one's outdoor sojourns in this region.

This is also the part of the state where the greatest populations of alligators live. Unlike anoles, which threaten but can't back it up, alligators are nonchalant creatures that rarely appear better than comatose, but they are genuinely deadly if crossed. All along river and creek banks, bays, and swamps, you'll see their scaly hulks basking motionless in the sun. While canoeing or kayaking, you might only be able to see the little arcs of their eyes and nostrils poking out from underwater, and maybe the scaly ridges of their backs and tails. They may just as easily be totally submerged, floating underwater and thinking sinister thoughts. Be careful where you step, and avoid wading or swimming in fresh water. Above all, keep small children and pets well clear of anywhere a gator might lurk. That said, alligators are some of the most thrillingly strange animals to be found anywhere in the United States, and the herp-fancier, against better judgment, is bound to find them brutishly lovable.

In certain, highly specialized environments—mainly in and around Carolina bays that offer both moistness and nutrient-poor soil—the Venus flytrap and other carnivorous plants thrive. To the average fly, these are more threatening than an alligator any day. The flytrap and some of its cousins are endangered, but in this region—and nowhere else in the world—you'll have plenty of opportunities to see them growing and gorging.

KURE BEACH

Kure is a two-syllable name: pronounced "Kyur-ee" (as in Madame, but not "curry"). This is a small beach community, not an extravaganza of neon lights and shark-doored towel shops. Most of the buildings on the

Kure Beach

© CAPE FEAR CVB

island are houses, both rental houses for vacationers and the homes of Kure Beach's year-round residents. The beach itself, like all North Carolina ocean beaches, is public.

Carolina Beach State Park

Just to the north of Kure is Carolina Beach State Park (1010 State Park Rd. off of 421, Carolina Beach, 910/458-8206, www.ncparks .gov/Visit/parks/cabe/main.php). Of all the state parks in the coastal region, this may be the one with the greatest ecological diversity. Within its boundaries are coastal pine and oak forests, pocosins between the dunes, saltwater marshes, a 50-foot sand dune, and limesink ponds; of the limesink ponds, one is a deep cypress swamp, one is a natural garden of water lilies, and one an ephemeral pond that dries into a swampy field every year, an ideal home for the many carnivorous plants that live here. You'll see Venus flytraps and their ferocious cousins here, but please resist the urge to dig or pick them, or to tempt them with your fingertips. Sort of like stinging insects that die after delivering their payload, the flytraps' traps can wither and fall off once they're sprung.

The park has 83 drive-to/walk-in campsites, each with a grill and picnic table. Two are wheelchair-accessible. Restrooms and hot showers are nearby. Camping is $15 per night, $10 per night for campers over the age of 62.

Fort Fisher State Park

At the southern end of Kure Beach is Fort Fisher State Park (1000 Loggerhead Rd. off U.S. 421, 910/458-5798, www.ncparks.gov/ Visit/parks/fofi/main.php, 8 A.M.–9 P.M. June– Aug., 8 A.M.–8 P.M. Mar.–May and Sept.–Oct., 8 A.M.–6 P.M. Nov.–Feb.). Fort Fisher has six miles of beautiful beach, a less crowded and commercial alternative to the other beaches of the area. A lifeguard is on duty between Memorial Day and Labor Day from 10 A.M.– 5:45 P.M. The park also includes a 1.1-mile hiking trail that winds through marshes and along the sound, ending at an observation deck where visitors can watch wildlife.

This is also a significant historic site. Fort Fisher was a Civil War earthwork stronghold designed to withstand massive assault. Modeled in part upon the Crimean War's Tower of Malakhoff, Fort Fisher's construction was an epic saga in itself, as hundreds of Confederate soldiers, African American slaves, and conscripted Lumbee Indians were brought in to build what became the Confederacy's largest fort. After the fall of Norfolk in 1862, Wilmington became the most important open port in the South, a vital harbor for blockade-runners and military vessels. Fisher held until nearly the end of the War. On Christmas Eve of 1864, U.S. General Benjamin "The Beast" Butler attacked the fort with 1,000 men, but was repulsed—a retreat that led to his being relieved of his command. A few weeks later, in January 1865, Fort Fisher was finally taken, but it required a Yankee force of 9,000 men and 56 ships in what was to be the largest amphibious assault until World War II. Without its defenses at Fort Fisher, Wilmington soon fell, hastening the end of the war, which came only three months later. Thanks to the final assault by the Union forces, and a century and a half of subsequent winds, tides, and hurricanes, not a great deal of the massive earthworks survives. But the remains of this vitally important Civil War site are preserved in an oddly peaceful and pretty seaside park, which contains a restored gun emplacement and a visitors center with interpretive exhibits.

Also at Fort Fisher is a branch of the **North Carolina Aquarium** (910/458-8257, 9 A.M.–5 P.M. daily year-round, until 9 P.M. Thurs. in summer, $8 adults, $7 seniors, $6 under 17). Like its sisters at Roanoke and Pine Knoll Shores, this is a beautiful aquarium that specializes in the native marine life of the North Carolina waters. It's also a center for marine biology and conservation efforts, assisting in the rescue and rehabilitation of sea turtles, marine mammals, freshwater reptiles, and other creatures of the coast. While at the Aquarium, be sure to visit the albino alligator.

Accommodations

The beaches of the Carolinas used to be lined

with boarding houses, the old-time choice in lodging for generations of middle-class tourists. They were sort of a precursor to today's bed-and-breakfasts, cozy family homes where visitors dined together with the hosts and were treated not so much like customers as houseguests—which is just what they were. Hurricane Hazel razed countless guesthouses when it pummeled the coast in 1954, ushering in the next epoch, that of the family motel. The **Beacon House** (715 Carolina Beach Ave. N., 877/232-2666, www.beaconhouseinnb-b.com, breakfast not included, some pets permitted in cottages with an extra fee) at Carolina Beach, just north of Kure, is a rare survival from that era. The early-1950s boarding house has the typical upstairs and downstairs porches, and dark wood paneling indoors. (Nearby cottages are also rented by the Beacon House.) The price is much higher than it was in those days (now $150 and up in the high season, much less in the off-season), but you'll be treated to a lodging experience from a long-gone era.

BALD HEAD ISLAND

Bald Head Island, an exclusive community where golf carts are the only traffic, is a two-mile, 20-minute ferry ride from Southport. More than eighty percent of the island is designated as a nature preserve, and at the southern tip stands "Old Baldy," the oldest lighthouse in North Carolina.

Sights

The **Bald Head Island Lighthouse** (910/457-5003, www.oldbaldy.org, 10 A.M.–4 P.M. Tues.–Sat., 11 A.M.–4 P.M. Sun., call for winter hours, $3 to climb) was built in 1818, replacing an even earlier tower that was completed in 1795. Despite being the newcomer at Bald Head, the 109-foot lighthouse is the oldest such structure surviving in North Carolina. A visit to the lighthouse includes a stop next door at the **Smith Island Museum** housed in the lighthouse keeper's home. The development of Smith Island (of which Bald Head is the terminus) allowed almost 17,000 acres to be set aside as an ecological preserve. The Old Baldy

Bald Head Island Lighthouse

Foundation leads **historic tours** (910/457-5003, 10:30 A.M. Tues.–Sat., $40, $30 guests of island establishments) of Bald Head, departing from Island Ferry Landing, a short walk from the lighthouse.

Food

A popular eatery on Bald Head is **Eb and Flo's Steam Bar** (910/457-7217, closed Wed. and in the winter, $10–20). It's on the waterfront, with the lighthouse behind it and a dining room/deck view over Long Bay to Fort Caswell. The seafood steamer pot is the specialty, and there is also a selection of burgers and sandwiches.

At Carolina Beach the **Shuckin' Shack** (6 N. Lake Park Blvd., 910/458-7380, www .pleasureislandoysterbar.com, Mon.–Sat. 11 A.M.–midnight, Sun. noon–midnight) is a friendly little oyster bar that serves fresh local seafood, and oysters by the bucket. After a meal at the Shuckin' Shack, stop by **Britt's Donuts** (11 Boardwalk, no phone number, www.carolina beach.net/britts1.html, reopening spring 2010, summer hours 8:30 A.M.–10:30 P.M. daily).

Britts has been famous for its homemade do-nuts since opening its doors in 1939.

SOUTHPORT

Without a doubt one of North Carolina's prettiest towns, Southport is an 18th-century river town whose port was overtaken by Wilmington in importance—and hence it has remained small and quiet. It was the Brunswick County seat until the late 1970s, when that job was outsourced to Bolivia. (Bolivia, North Carolina, that is.) There have been plans in the works for the construction of an enormous international port here, and should that ever come to pass, this peaceful riverbank will be irrevocably changed. Given Southport's history—which has included several eras when the town seemed just on the brink of large-scale growth and importance in the world of international trade—it may be that the North Carolina International Port will go the way of Southport's other pipe dreams. In the meantime, it's a wonderfully charming place, with block upon block of beautiful historic houses and public buildings. The old cemetery is a gorgeous spot, and in it you'll find many tombstones that bear witness to the town's seafaring history—epitaphs for sea captains who died while visiting Smithville (Southport's original name), and stones carved with pictures of ships on rolling waves.

Sights

The **North Carolina Maritime Museum at Southport** (116 N. Howe St., 910/457-0003, www.ncmaritime.org/branches/southport_default.htm, 9 A.M.–5 P.M. Mon.–Fri., 10 A.M.–5 P.M. Sat., and 1–5 P.M. Sun., $2 adults, $1 over 62, free under 16) is a smaller, storefront branch of the Maritime Museum at Beaufort, where you can learn about the seafaring history of the Carolina coast. Among the many topics of interest here is the life of pirate Stede Bonnet, whose girly surname belies his infamous life of crime. Bonnet, who spent much time in the Southport area, was by turns the pillaging buddy and bitter rival of Blackbeard. Other cool displays in the museum include a section of a 2,000-year-old,

54-inch Indian canoe, and an 8-foot jawbone of a whale.

Events

Southport hosts the state's best-known **Fourth of July celebration** (910/457-6964, www.nc4thofjuly.com), attended each year by up to 50,000 people. (That's approximately 20 times the normal population of the town.) In addition to the requisite fireworks, food, and music, the festival features a special tribute to veterans, a flag retirement ceremony (that is, folks bring their old and worn-out flags), and a naturalization ceremony for new Americans.

Shopping

There are two pet boutiques in Southport, where you can pick up treats for your canine traveling companion or presents to bring back to your pets at home. **Zeetlegoo's Pet and People Store** (1635 N. Howe St., 910/457-5663, www.zeetlegoo.com, 10 A.M.–6 P.M. Mon.–Fri., 10 A.M.–4 P.M. Sat.) sells toys and treats for cats, dogs, and exotics, as well as leashes, cat furniture, and health products. Timber, a golden retriever mix, and Sammy, a cream-colored cat, are the resident product testers. **Cool Dogs & Crazy Cats** (310 N. Howe St., 910/457-0115, www.cooldogscrazycats.com) has a selection of fresh-baked biscuit delicacies, organic catnip, supplies and toys for cats and dogs, and jewelry and other items for their human customers.

Accommodations

Lois Jane's Riverview Inn (106 W. Bay St., 800/457-1152, www.loisjanes.com, $93–143 depending on season) is a Victorian waterfront home built by the innkeeper's grandfather. The rooms are comfortably furnished, bright and not frou-frou, and the Queen Deluxe Street, a cottage behind the inn, has its own kitchen and separate entrance. The front porch of the inn gives a wonderful view of the harbor. At the same location is the **Riverside Motel** (106 W. Bay St., 910/457-6986, www.riversidemotelinc.com, $65–75), which also has a front porch with a fantastic panorama of the shipping channel. Another affordable option is the **Inn at River Oaks** (512 N. Howe St., 910/457-1100, www.theinnatriveroaks.com, $65–135), a motel-style inn with very simple suites.

The **Inn at South Harbour Village** (South Harbour Village, 800/454-0815, www.south harbourvillageinn.com, $120–370, two-night minimum in high season) is a waterfront hotel in a development between Southport and Oak Island. The nine condo-style luxury suites have efficiency kitchens and dining rooms, inviting extended stays. The property overlooks the Intracoastal Waterway and South Harbour marina.

At Oak Island, west of Southport, **Captain's Cove Motel** (6401 E. Oak Island Dr., Oak Island, 910/278-6026, www.realpages.com/captainscove, avg. $65) is a long-established family motel one block from the beach. The **Island Resort and Inn** (500 Ocean Dr., Oak Island, 910/278-5644, www.islandresortand inn.com, $75–190 depending on season) is a beachfront property with standard motel rooms and one- and two-bedroom apartment suites. The **Ocean Crest Motel** (1417 East Beach Dr., Oak Island, 910/278-3333, www.ocean-crest-motel.com, $65–155 depending on season) is a large condo-style motel, also right on the beach.

Food

The 🍸 **Yacht Basin Provision Company** (130 Yacht Basin St., 910/457-0654, $10–20) is a Southport seafood joint with a super-casual atmosphere. Customers place their orders at the counter and serve themselves drinks (on an honor system), then seat themselves dockside to await the arrival of their chow. Most popular here are the conch fritters and grouper salad sandwich, but anything you order will be good.

OCEAN ISLE

Ocean Isle is the next-to-most-southerly beach in North Carolina, separated from South Carolina only by Bird Island and the town of Calabash. In October, Ocean Isle is the site of the **North Carolina Oyster Festival** (www.brunswick countychamber.org/OF-nc-oyster-festival.cfm), a huge event that's been happening for nearly

30 years. In addition to an oyster stew cook-off, surfing competition, and entertainment, this event features the North Carolina Oyster Shucking Competition. Oyster shucking is not so picayune a skill as it might sound. In the not-that-long-ago days when North Carolina's seafood industry was ascendant, workers—most often African American women—lined up on either side of long work tables in countless oyster houses along the coast and the creeks, and opened and cut out thousands of oysters a day. A complex occupational culture was at work in those rooms, one that had its own vocabulary, stories, and songs. The speed at which these women worked was a source of collective and individual pride, and the fastest shuckers enjoyed quite a bit of prestige among their colleagues. High-speed shucking is a skill that's well remembered by many Carolinians who might now be working at Wal-Mart, rather than in the old dockside shacks and warehouses. The state shucking championship is the time when some of the best shuckers prove that although North Carolina may have changed around them, they haven't missed a beat.

SOUTH ALONG U.S. 17

U.S. 17 is an old colonial road—in fact, its original name, still used in some stretches, is the King's Highway. George Washington passed this way on his 1791 Southern tour, staying with the prominent planters of this area and leaving in his wake the proverbial legends about where he lay his head of an evening. Today, the King's Highway, following roughly its original course, is still the main thoroughfare through Brunswick County into South Carolina.

🍸 Orton Plantation

Gardens adorn the relentlessly beautiful grounds of an early 18th-century rice plantation (9149 Orton Rd. SE, Winnabow, 910/371-6851, www.ortongardens.com, 8 A.M.–6 P.M. spring and summer, 10 A.M.–5 P.M. fall and winter, closed Dec.–Feb., $9 adults, $8 seniors, $3 children). The centerpiece of the estate is the 1735 house, with circa-1840 additions; it's a quintessential white-columned antebellum palace, and a dead-ringer for *Gone with the Wind*'s Twelve Oaks. (The house is still a home, and is not open to the public.) A tragic history underlies the plantation's beauty, beginning with the extermination of the local native tribe that tried to repulse white encroachment by destroying the first house on this site. The Lowcountry rice plantation was one of the most complex, labor-intensive kinds of antebellum industry, and Orton, no exception, was home to a large slave community. Yankees occupied it during the Civil War and used the house as a hospital. This was a blessing in disguise, as it probably saved the house from being burned, the fate of many of the other great plantations along and near the King's Highway.

It was in the early 20th century that the formal gardens came into being, the project of Mrs. Luola Sprunt. Many of the massive live oaks, which look like they've been here for centuries, were actually planted in this era. Orton is perhaps the state's most famous azalea garden, an amazing spectacle of color in the gentle Lowcountry springtime. Swamps and river marshes sidle up to the gardens, and are home to many species of water birds, and—mind

where you walk along the water's edge—a population of fat and happy alligators.

Brunswick Town and Fort Anderson

Nearby to Orton is the **Brunswick Town/ Fort Anderson State Historic Site** (8884 St. Philip's Rd. SE, Winnabow, 910/371-6613, www.ah.dcr.state.nc.us/sections/hs/brunswic/brunswic.htm, 10 A.M.–4 P.M. Tues.–Sat.), the site of what was a bustling little port town in the early and mid-1700s. In its brief life, Brunswick saw quite a bit of action. It was attacked in 1748 by a Spanish ship, which, to residents' delight, blew up in the river. (One of that ship's cannons was dragged out of the river about 20 years ago and is on display here.) In 1765, the town's refusal to observe royal tax stamps was a successful precursor to the Boston Tea Party eight years later. But by the end of the Revolutionary War, Brunswick Town was solid gone, burned by the British but having been made obsolete anyway by the growth of Wilmington. Today nothing remains of the colonial port except for the lovely ruins of the 1754 **St. Philip's Anglican Church** and some

© SARAH BRYAN

The ruins of the 1754 St. Philip's Anglican Church are among the few vestiges of Brunswick Town.

building foundations uncovered by archaeologists. During the Civil War, Fort Anderson was built upon this site, sand earthworks that were part of the crucial defenses of the Cape Fear, protecting the blockade-runners who came and went from Wilmington. Some of the walls of that fort also survive. A visitors center at the historic site tells the story of this surprisingly significant stretch of riverbank, and the grounds, with the town's foundations exposed and interpreted, are an intriguing vestige of a forgotten community.

Nature Preserves

The Nature Conservancy's **Green Swamp Preserve** (NC 211, 5.5 miles north of Supply, Nature Conservancy regional office 910/395-5000, www.nature.org/wherewework/north america/states/northcarolina/preserves/art 5606.html) contains nearly 16,000 acres of some of North Carolina's most precious coastal ecosystems, the longleaf pine savanna and evergreen shrub pocosin. Hiking is allowed in the preserve, but the paths are primitive. It's important to stay on the trails and not explore in the wilds because this is an intensely fragile ecosystem. In this preserve are communities of rare carnivorous plants, including the monstrous little pink-mawed Venus flytrap, four kinds of pitcher plant, and sticky-fingered sundew. It's also a habitat for the rare red-cockaded woodpecker, which is partial to diseased, old-growth longleaf pines as a place to call home.

The Nature Conservancy maintains another nature preserve nearby, the **Boiling Spring Lakes Preserve** (off of NC 87, Boiling Spring Lakes, trail begins at Community Center, Nature Conservancy regional office 910/395-5000, www.nature.org/wherewe work/northamerica/states/northcarolina/preserves/art12787.html). Brunswick County contains the state's greatest concentration of rare plant species, and the most diverse plant communities anywhere on the East Coast north of Florida. This preserve is owned by the Plant Conservation Program, and includes

over half the acreage of the town of Boiling Spring Lakes. The ecosystem here is made up of Carolina bays, pocosins, and longleaf pine forests. Like the Green Swamp Preserve, many of the species here are dependent on periodic fires in order to propagate and survive. The Nature Conservancy does controlled burning at both sites to maintain this rare habitat.

Calabash and Vicinity

The once tiny fishing village of Calabash, just above the South Carolina line, was founded in the early 18th century as Pea Landing, a shipping point for the bounteous local peanut crop. Calabashes, a kind of gourd, were used as dippers in the town supply of drinking water, and when the settlement was renamed in 1873, it was supposedly for that reason that it became Calabash.

In the early 1940s, a style of restaurant seafood was developed here that involves deep-frying lightly battered fish and shellfish. As the style caught on and more restaurants were built here, the term "Calabash-style seafood" was born. Jimmy Durante was fond of dining in Calabash, and some will claim that it was in tribute to food here that he signed off on his shows saying, "Good night, Mrs. Calabash, wherever you are." Though Calabash seafood is advertised at restaurants all over the country now, this little town has more than enough restaurants of its own to handle the yearly onslaught of tourists in search of an authentic Calabash meal. Local favorite spots for seafood are the **Calabash Seafood Hut** (1125 River Rd., 910/579-6723, 11 A.M.–9 P.M. daily), and, right on the docks, **Dockside Seafood House** (9955 Nance St. SW, 910/579-6775).

Indigo Farms (1542 Hickman Rd. NW, Calabash, 910/287-6794, www.indigofarms market.com, 8 A.M.–5 P.M. Mon.–Sat., longer in the warm months), three miles above the South Carolina line in Calabash, is a superb farm market, selling all manner of produce, preserves, and baked goods. They also have corn mazes and farm activities in the fall, and are a training site for porcine contestants in the prestigious local NASPIG races.

Sunset Beach, the southernmost of the Brunswick County beaches, is a wonderfully small-time place, a cozy town that until 2008 could only be reached via a one-lane pontoon bridge. One of the area's most popular restaurants is located just on the inland side of the bridge to Sunset Beach. **Twin Lakes Seafood Restaurant** (102 Sunset Blvd., 910/579-6373, http://twinlakesseafood.com) was built almost 40 years ago by Clarice and Ronnie Holden, both natives of the area. Clarice was born into a cooking family, the daughter of one of the founders of the Calabash restaurant tradition. Twin Lakes serves fresh, locally caught seafood, a rarity in this time and place. In-season and on weekends, expect long lines.

In the nearby town of Shallotte (pronounced "Shuh-LOTE"), **Holden Brothers Farm Market** (5600 Ocean Hwy. W., 910/579-4500) is a popular source for local produce. The peaches in season are wonderful, and the variety of homemade canned goods and pickles are worth the trip.

GETTING THERE AND AROUND

The Brunswick County beaches like Holden, Ocean Isle, and Sunset are an easy drive on U.S. 17. The beaches and islands along the Cape itself, due south of Wilmington, are not as close to 17. They can be reached by taking U.S. 76 south from the city, or by ferry from Southport. The **Southport-Fort Fisher Ferry** (800/293-3779 or 800/368-8969) is popular as a sightseeing jaunt as well as a means simply to get across the river. It's a 30-minute crossing; most departures are 45 minutes apart, 5:30 A.M.–7:45 P.M. from Southport (until 6:15 P.M. in the winter), and 6:15 A.M.–8:30 P.M. leaving Fort Fisher (until 7 P.M. in the winter). For most vehicles, the fare is $5, but if you're driving a rig that's more than 20 feet long, boat trailers and the like included, the price can be as high as $15. It's $1 for pedestrians, $2 for bicycle riders, and $3 for folks on motorcycle. Pets are permitted if leashed or in a vehicle, and there are bathrooms on all ferries.

© SARAH BRYAN

One of North Carolina's public ferries runs all year between Fort Fisher and Southport.

Points Inland from Wilmington

Moving inland from the Wilmington area, you will pass first through a lush world of wetlands distinguished by the peculiar Carolina bays. Not necessarily bodies of water, as the name would suggest, the bays are actually ovoid depressions in the earth, of unknown and much-debated origin. They are often water-filled, but by definition are fed by rainwater rather than creeks or groundwater. They create unique environments, and are often surrounded by bay laurels (hence the name), and guarded by a variety of carnivorous plants.

The next zone, bounded by the Waccamaw and Lumber Rivers, is largely made up of farmland and small towns. This was for generations prime tobacco country, and that heritage is still very much evident in towns like Whiteville, where old tobacco warehouses line the railroad tracks. Culturally, this area—mostly in Columbus County, extending a little ways into Robeson to the west and Brunswick to the east—is of a piece with the three counties in South Carolina with which it shares a border—Horry, Marion, and Dillon. Many of the same family names are still to be found on either side of the state line.

The area around the Lumber River, especially in Robeson County, is the home of the Lumbee, native people with an amazing heritage of devotion to faith and family, and steadfast resistance to oppression. If you turn on the radio while driving through this area, you'll likely find Lumbee gospel programming, and get a sense of the cadences of Lumbee English. The characteristics that make it different from the speech of local whites and African Americans are very subtle, but certain hallmarks of pronunciation and grammar (which include the sub-variations of different families and towns within the community) distinguish the tribe's speech as one of the state's most distinctive dialects.

At the edge of the region is Fayetteville. From its early days as the center of Cape Fear Scottish settlement to its current role as one of

the most important military communities in the United States, Fayetteville has always been one of the most significant of North Carolina's cities.

ALONG HIGHWAY 74

A little ways inland from Calabash, the countryside is threaded by the Waccamaw River, a gorgeous, dark channel full of cypress knees and dangerous reptiles. (The name is pronounced "WAW-cuh-MAW," with slightly more emphasis on the first syllable than the third.) It winds its way down from Lake Waccamaw through a swampy little portion of North Carolina, crossing Horry County, South Carolina (unofficial motto: "The H is silent"), before joining its fellow North Carolina natives, the Pee Dee and Lumber Rivers, to let out in Winyah Bay at the colonial port of Georgetown. Through the little toenail of North Carolina that the Waccamaw crosses, it parallels the much longer Lumber River, surrounding the very rural Columbus County and

swamp landscape near Pembroke

© SARAH BRYAN

part of Robeson County in an environment of deep, subtropical wetlands.

Sights

Pembroke is the town around which much of the Lumbee community revolves, and at the center of life here is the University of North Carolina at Pembroke. Founded in 1887 as the Indian Normal School, UNCP's population is now only about one-quarter Native American, but it's still an important site in North Carolina's native history. The **Museum of the Native American Resource Center** (Old Main, UNCP, 910/521-6282, www.uncp .edu/nativemuseum, 8 A.M.–noon and 1–5 P.M. Mon.–Sat., free) is on campus, occupying Old Main, a 1923 building that's a source of pride for the Pembroke community. The Resource Center has a small but very good collection of old artifacts and contemporary art by members of Native American tribes across the country.

Laurinburg's **John Blue House** (13040 X-way Rd., 910/276-2495, www.johnblue cottonfestival.com) is a spectacle of Victorian design, a polygonal house built entirely of heart pine harvested from the surrounding property, and done up like a wedding cake with endless decorative devices. John Blue, the builder and original owner, was an inventor of machinery used in the processing of cotton. A pre–Civil War cotton gin stands on the property, and is used for educational demonstrations throughout the year. This is the site of the **John Blue Cotton Festival,** an October event that showcases not only the ingenuity of the home's famous resident, and the process of ginning cotton, but also lots of local and regional musicians and other artists.

◖ Strike at the Wind

For more than 30 years, the Lumbee tribe has put on a production of the play *Strike at the Wind* (North Carolina Indian Cultural Center, 638 Terry Sanford Rd., Pembroke, 910/521-0835,

HENRY BERRY LOWRY

In some places, the Civil War didn't end the day Lee surrendered, but smoldered on in terrible local violence. One such place was the Lumbee community of Robeson County, in the days of the famous Lowry Band.

Then as now, Lowry (also spelled Lowrie) was a prominent name in the tribe. During the Civil War, Allen Lowry led a band of men who hid out in the swamps, eluding conscription into the backbreaking corps of semi-slave labor that was forced to build earthenworks to defend Wilmington. When the war ended, violence against the Lumbees continued, and the Lowry Band retaliated, attacking the plantations of their wartime pursuers. Allen Lowry and his oldest son were captured in 1865 and executed. Henry Berry Lowry, the youngest son, inherited the mantle of leadership.

For the next several years, long after the end of the Civil War, the Lowry Band was pursued relentlessly. Arrested and imprisoned, Lowry and his band escaped from prison in Lumberton and Wilmington. Between 1868 and 1872, the state and federal governments tried everything – putting a bounty on Lowry's head, even sending in a federal artillery battalion. After an 11-month campaign of unsuccessful pursuit, the federal soldiers gave up. Soon afterwards, the Lowry Band emerged from the swamps, raided Lumberton, and made off with a large amount of money. This was the end of the road for the Lowry Band, though, and one by one its members were all killed in 1872 – except, perhaps, Henry Berry. It's unknown whether he died, went back into hiding, or left the area altogether. As befits a legend, he seems simply to have disappeared.

Henry Berry Lowry is a source of fierce pride to modern Lumbees, a symbol of the tribe's resistance and resilience. Every summer, members of the tribe perform in the long-running outdoor drama *Strike at the Wind,* which tells the story of the Lowry Band. Another vivid retelling of the story is the 2001 novel *Nowhere Else on Earth,* by Josephine Humphreys.

www.strikeatthewind.com, July 7–Aug. 26, Fri. and Sat., show begins at 8 P.M., play at 8:30 P.M., $12 adults, $6 ages 6–13 and over 61, $2 parking), which takes place in the outdoor Adolph Dial Amphitheater on the banks of the Lumber River. (Adolph Dial was one of the greatest scholars of Lumbee history.) The play, which tells the story of Henry Berry Lowry and his gang, is acted by members of the Lumbee tribe, as well as white and African American cast members, and while a few of the cast are professional actors, most are people from the surrounding area who are simply passionate about their history and want to be part of its most famous public portrait. The music for the play was composed by songwriter Willie French Lowery, himself an important artistic ambassador of the Lumbee tribe.

Entertainment and Events

Several of the state's big agricultural festivals are held in this area. If you're in the little town of Fair Bluff in late July, you might be lucky enough to witness the coronation of the newest Watermelon Queen. The **North Carolina Watermelon Festival** (910/641-7442, www.ncwatermelonfestival.com) began as an annual competition between two friends, local farmers whose watermelons grew to over 100 pounds. The two-man competition expanded into this festival that celebrates watermelon-growing throughout the state, and in which a new court of watermelon royalty is crowned every year.

In Tabor City, there's a famous **Yam Festival** (910/840-0292 www.discover columbuscounty.org) in October, during which the tiny town's population sometimes quadruples. Yam partisans crown their own royal court during this festival. Then when spring rolls back around, Chadbourn holds its annual **Strawberry Festival** (www.ncstrawberry festival.com), at which the coronation of the Strawberry Queen takes place. If this seems a strange sort of royalty, bear in mind that across the South Carolina line, they have a Little Miss Hell Hole Swamp competition.

All of North Carolina, and in particular the Cape Fear region in the southeast, has a great deal of Scottish ancestry and heritage. In the small town of Red Springs in Robeson County, a small Presbyterian school, Flora Macdonald College, operated for many years. Though it's now been closed for a generation, its grounds and lovely gardens are listed in the National Register of Historic Places and are the setting of the annual **Flora Macdonald Highland Games** (200 South College St., Red Springs, 910/843-5000, www.capefearscots.com). Like its counterpart to the west at Grandfather Mountain, these Highland Games are a fun celebration of Celtic culture. The festival includes piping competitions, sheepdog competitions, food, dancing, and of course the traditional feats of highland athleticism like tossing the caber.

Sports and Recreation

Several beautiful state parks line the Waccamaw and Lumber Rivers. **Lake Waccamaw State Park** (1866 State Park Dr., Lake Waccamaw, 910/646-4748, http://ncparks.gov/Visit/parks/lawa/main.php, park office open 8 A.M.–5 P.M. daily, 8 A.M.–6 P.M. Nov.–Apr., 8 A.M.–8 P.M. Mar.–May, 8 A.M.–9 P.M. June–Aug., 8 A.M.–8 P.M. Sept. and Oct.) encompasses the 9,000-acre lake of that name. The lake is technically a Carolina bay, a mysterious geological feature of this region. Carolina bays are large, oval depressions in the ground, many of which are boggy and filled with water, but which are actually so-named because of the bay trees that typically grow in and around them. Lake Waccamaw has geological and hydrological characteristics that make it unique even within the odd enough category of Carolina bays. Because of its proximity to a large limestone deposit, the water is more neutral than its usually very acidic cousins, and so it supports a greater diversity of life. There are several aquatic creatures that live only here, with great names like the Waccamaw fatmucket and silverside (a mollusk and a fish, respectively). The park draws many boaters and paddlers, naturally, though the only available launches are outside the property. Primitive campsites are available in the park for $9/night.

North of Whiteville on Highway 701 is Elizabethtown, location of **Jones Lake State Park** (4117 Hwy. 242, Elizabethtown, 910/588-4550, www.ncparks.gov/Visit/parks/jone/main.php, park office open 8 A.M.–5 P.M. weekdays, park open 8 A.M.–6 P.M. Nov.–Feb., 8 A.M.–8 P.M. Mar.–May, 8 A.M.–9 P.M. June–Aug., 8 A.M.–8 P.M. Sept. and Oct.). Visitors can go boating on Jones Lake, either in their own craft (no motors over 10 horsepower), or in canoes or paddleboats rented from the park at $5/hour, $3 for each additional hour. The lake is also great for swimming, between Memorial Day and Labor Day, with shallow, cool water and a sandy beach. There are a concession stand and bathhouse at the beach, and swimming costs $4/day for visitors 13 and over, $3/day ages 3–12. Camping is available in a wooded area, with drinking water and restrooms nearby. Visit the park's website for the rather complicated pricing system.

Singletary Lake State Park (6707 Hwy. 53 E., Kelly, 910/669-2928, www.ncparks .gov/Visit/parks/sila/main.php), north of Lake Waccamaw in Kelly, centers around one of the largest of the Carolina bays, the 572-acre Singletary Lake, which lies within the Bladen Lakes State Forest. There is no individual camping here, though there are facilities for large groups—including the entrancingly named Camp Ipecac—which date from the Civilian Conservation Corps era. There is a nice one-mile hiking trail, the CCC-Carolina Bay Loop Trail, and a 500-foot pier extending over the bay. Some of the cypress trees here are estimated to have been saplings when the first Englishmen set foot on Roanoke Island.

Lumber River State Park (2819 Princess Ann Rd., Orrum, 910/628-4564, http://nc-parks.gov/Visit/parks/luri/main.php) has 115 miles of waterways, with numerous put-ins for canoes and kayaks. The river, referred to as the Lumber or Lumbee River, or, in areas farther upstream, as Drowning Creek, traverses both the coastal plain region and the eastern edge of the Sandhills. Camping is available here

for $9 per night at unimproved walk-in and canoe-in sites.

Yogi Bear's Jellystone Park (626 Richard Wright Rd., 877/668-8586, www.taborcity jellystone.com), formerly known as Daddy Joe's, is a popular campground with RV and tent spaces, rental cabins, and yurts. The facilities are clean and well maintained, and there are tons of children's activities on-site. Some of the camping is in wooded areas, but for the most part expect direct sun and plan accordingly.

In Fair Bluff is **River Bend Outfitters** (1206 Main St., 910/649-5998, www.white villenc.com/rbo), a canoe and kayak company that specializes in paddling and camping trips along the beautiful blackwater Lumber River.

Food

In an old hotel on the shore of Lake Waccamaw is **Dale's Seafood** (100 Canal Cove Rd., Lake Waccamaw, 910/646-4466, 11 A.M.–9 P.M. Mon.–Thurs., 11 A.M.–9:30 P.M. Fri. and Sat.). Dale's is a local favorite, specializing in Calabash-style seafood.

If you pass through Tabor City, don't neglect to have a meal at the █ **Todd House** (102 Live Oak St., 910/653-3778, www.todd-house.com), which has been serving fine country cooking since 1923. The Todds are one of the oldest families in the area along the state line, and the first in the restaurant business was Mrs. Mary Todd, who took to cooking meals for visiting tobacco buyers. (This area lived and died by tobacco for generations.) Through her daughter's time, and a couple of subsequent owners, the Todd House has continued to serve famously good barbecue, fried chicken, and other down-home specialties. Their wonderful pies are available for purchase, so pick one up for the road.

There's a take-out counter in Whiteville that chowhounds will drive an hour out of their way to reach, because it's said to have the best burgers anywhere around. Next to the railroad tracks, **Ward's Grill** (706 S. Madison St., 910/642-2004, 7 A.M.–2 P.M. Mon.–Thurs., 7 A.M.–1 P.M. Wed., 7 A.M.–12 P.M. first two Saturdays of the month) has no seating, just a walk-up counter. Its burgers are famous, as are its chili dogs.

In Lumberton, try **Fuller's Old-Fashion BBQ** (3201 Roberts Ave., Lumberton, 910/738-8694, www.fullersbbq.com, 11 A.M.–9 P.M. Mon.–Sat., 11 A.M.–4 P.M. Sun., lunch buffet $6.95, dinner buffet $9.50). Fuller's has a great reputation for its barbeque, but it also makes all sorts of country specialties like chicken gizzards and chitterlings, and a special twelve-layer cake.

Getting There and Around

This section of Southeastern North Carolina is bisected by I-95, the largest highway on the East Coast. I-95 passes right outside both Fayetteville and Lumberton. Major east-west routes include U.S. 74, which crosses the Cape Fear at Wilmington and proceeds through Lake Waccamaw and Whiteville to pass just south of Lumberton and Pembroke, going to Laurinburg. N.C. 87 goes through Elizabethtown, where you can choose to branch off onto 211 to Lumberton, or bear north on N.C. 87 to Fayetteville.

FAYETTEVILLE

Fayetteville is North Carolina's sixth-largest city, and in its own quiet way has always been one of the state's most powerful engines of growth and change. In the early 1700s, it became a hub for settlement by Scottish immigrants, who helped build it into a major commercial center. From the 1818 initiation of steamboat travel between Fayetteville and Wilmington along the Cape Fear—initially a voyage of six days!—to the building of the Plank Road, a huge boon to intrastate commerce, Fayetteville was well connected to commercial resources all through the Carolinas.

At a national level, Fayetteville serves as the location of two high-level military installations. Fort Bragg is the home of the XVIII Airborne Corps, the 82nd Airborne, the Delta Force, and the John F. Kennedy Special Warfare Center and School. As such, it's also the home of many widows and children of soldiers who have died in Iraq and Afghanistan.

Pope Air Force Base is nearby, the home of the 43rd Airlift Wing, and its Maintenance, Support, and Operations Groups.

Sights

The **Museum of the Cape Fear Regional Complex** (801 Arsenal Ave., 910/486-1330, http://ncmuseumofhistory.org/osm/mcf.html, 10 A.M.–5 P.M. Tues.–Sat., 1–5 P.M. Sun.) has three components, each telling different stories of Fayetteville's history. The museum itself has exhibits on the history and prehistory of the region, including its vital role in developing transportation in the state, as well as its centrality as a military center. There is an 1897 house museum, the Poe House, which belonged to a Mr. Edgar Allen Poe—not Edgar Allan the writer, but Edgar Allen, a brickyard owner. The third section is the 4.5-acre Arsenal Park, the site of a federal arms magazine built in 1836, claimed by the Confederacy in 1861, and destroyed by General Sherman in 1865.

The **Airborne and Special Operations Museum** (100 Bragg Blvd., 910/643-2766, www.asomf.org, 10 A.M.–5 P.M. Tues.–Sat., noon–5 P.M. Sun., closed Mon. except for federal holidays, free admission, $4 for theater and motion simulator) is an impressive facility that presents the history of Special Ops paratroopers, from the first jump in 1940 to the divisions' present-day roles abroad in peacekeeping missions and war. In the museum's theater you can watch an amazing film of what it looks like when a paratrooper makes the jump, and the 24-seat Pitch, Roll, and Yaw Vista-Dome Motion Simulator makes the experience even more exciting.

The **JFK Special Warfare Museum** (Building D-2502, Ardennes and Marion Sts., Fort Bragg, 910/432-4272, www.jfkwebstore .com/index.php, ID required to get onto the base) tells the story of further amazing facets of the U.S. military, including Special Ops and Psychological Ops. The museum focuses on the Vietnam War era, but chronicles unconventional warfare from colonial times to the present.

Going back a good bit further in time, the **Fayetteville Independent Light Infantry**

© J.ADAMS1

the Airborne and Special Operations Museum

Armory and Museum (210 Burgess St., 910/433-1612, open by appointment, free) displays artifacts from the history of the Light Infantry. The FILI is still active, dedicated as North Carolina's official historic military command, a ceremonial duty. But in its active-duty days, which began in 1793, FILI had some exciting times, particularly during the Civil War. In addition to the military artifacts, this museum also exhibits a carriage in which the Marquis de Lafayette was shown around Fayetteville—the only one of the towns bearing his name that he actually visited.

The 79-acre **Cape Fear Botanical Garden** (536 N. Eastern Blvd., 910/486-0221, www .capefearbg.org, 10 A.M.–5 P.M. Mon.–Sat., noon–5 P.M. Sun., closed Sun. mid-Dec.–Feb., $5 adults, $4 military and AAA, free under 12, everyone free first Sat. of every month and entire month of April) is one of the loveliest horticultural sites in North Carolina. The camellia and azalea gardens are spectacular sights in the early spring, but the variety of plantings and environments represented makes the whole

park a delight. Along the banks of the Paw Paw River and Cross Creek, visitors will find dozens of garden environments, from lily gardens and hosta gardens, to woods and a bog, and an 1880s farmhouse garden. Without a doubt, this is the prettiest place in Fayetteville.

Cross Creek Cemetery (North Cool Spring and Grove Sts., 800/255-8217, dawn–dusk daily) is an attractively sad spot, the resting place of many Scots men and women who crossed the ocean to settle the Cape Fear. Though people of all kinds and times are buried here, it is the oldest section that is most poignant, where one stone after another commemorates Mr. or Mrs. Mac-So-and-So, Late of Glasgow or Perth, Merchant in this Town. One can feel the invisible ties of kith and kin that led these early immigrants to band together for comfort in the New World. (While strolling this cemetery, and especially when pausing to read a stone, beware of extraordinarily fast-moving fire ants.)

Entertainment and Events

The **Cameo Theatre** (225 Hay St., 910/486-6633, www.cameoarthouse.com) is a cool old early-20th-century movie house, originally known as the New Dixie. Today it is "Fayetteville's alternative cinematic experience," a place for independent and art house movies.

The **Cape Fear Regional Theatre** (1209 Hay St., 910/323-4233, www.cfrt.org) began in 1962 as a tiny company with a bunch of borrowed equipment. Today it is a major regional theater with a wide reputation. Putting on several major productions each season, with a specialty of popular musicals, it draws actors and directors from around the country, but maintains its heart here in the Fayetteville arts community. The **Gilbert Theater** (116 Green St., entrance on Bow St., above Fascinate-U Museum, 910/678-7186, www.gilberttheater .com) is a small company that puts on a variety of productions throughout the year, with special emphasis on classic drama and multicultural offerings. Tickets are $10 and seating is on a first-come basis.

WILMINGTON AND CAPE FEAR

Fayetteville's late-April **Dogwood Festival** features rock, pop, and beach music bands; a dog show; a recycled art show; a "hogs and rags spring rally"; and the selection and coronation of Miss, Teen Miss, Young Miss, and Junior Miss Dogwood Festival.

Accommodations and Food

Fayetteville's lodging options are by and large chain motels, a multitude of which can be found at the Fayetteville exits off I-95. You'll generally find a pretty reasonable deal at the old standards, but if you'd like to stay somewhere with more personality, Wilmington and Raleigh are both easily accessible.

Likewise, the city's dining choices tend towards the highway chains. There are some exceptions, though. The 【 **Hilltop House** (1240 Fort Bragg Rd., 910/484-6699, www .hilltophousenc.com, lunch 11 A.M.–2 P.M. Mon.–Sat., supper 5–9 P.M. Mon.–Thurs. and 5–10 P.M. Fri. and Sat., Sun. brunch 10:30 A.M.–2:30 P.M., complimentary wine tasting every Tues. night, $15–25) serves hearty fare in an elegant setting, and was recognized in 2007 with a Wine Spectator Award for Excellence—not surprising, given that the Hilltop House has a 74-page wine list. More casual is the **Mash House** (4150 Sycamore Dairy Rd., 910/867-9223, www.themashhouse .com, $8–16), which has a good variety of pizzas and sandwiches, as well as heavier entrées and a selection of good homemade brews.

Information and Services

Cape Fear Valley Health Services (1638 Owen Dr., 910/615-4000, www.capefear valley.com) is a large hospital complex with acute care services, a major cardiac care program, and everything else one would expect from an important regional hospital.

The website of the **Fayetteville Area Convention and Visitors Bureau** (www.visit fayettevillenc.com) is an excellent source of tourist information for this city. There you'll find not only the basics about what, where, and how much, but detailed driving tours, extensive historical information, and much more.

Getting There and Around

Fayetteville Regional Airport (400 Airport Rd., 910/433-1160, flyfay.ci.fayetteville.nc.us) has daily flights to and from Charlotte (US Airways Express) and Atlanta (ASA, Delta Connections). The city is served by **Amtrak** (472 Hay St., 800/872-7245, www.amtrak .com, 10 A.M.–5:45 P.M. and 10 P.M.–5:45 A.M. daily) via the Palmetto and Silver Service lines. It's also a short hop off I-95. Fayetteville is also easily reached by N.C. 24, via Jacksonville, Warsaw, and Clinton.

www.moon.com

DESTINATIONS | ACTIVITIES | BLOGS | MAPS | BOOKS

MOON.COM is ready to help plan your next trip! Filled with fresh trip ideas and strategies, author interviews, informative travel blogs, a detailed map library, and descriptions of all the Moon guidebooks, Moon.com is all you need to get out and explore the world—or even places in your own backyard. While at Moon.com, sign up for our monthly e-newsletter for updates on new releases, travel tips, and expert advice from our on-the-go Moon authors. As always, when you travel with Moon, expect an experience that is uncommon and truly unique.

MOON IS ON FACEBOOK—BECOME A FAN!
JOIN THE MOON PHOTO GROUP ON FLICKR

MAP SYMBOLS

▬▬▬	Expressway	🄲	Highlight	✈	Airport	Ⓜ	Metro
▬▬▬	Primary Road	○	City/Town	✗	Airfield	🄿	Parking Area
▬▬▬	Secondary Road	◉	State Capital	▲	Mountain	♪	Golf Course
▭▭▭	Unpaved Road	⊛	National Capital	✦	Unique Natural Feature	⬕	Church
------	Trail	★	Point of Interest	⚐	Waterfall	⬛	Gas Station
··········	Ferry	•	Accommodation	⚑	Park	◠	Glacier
▬▬▬	Railroad	▼	Restaurant/Bar	⬛	Trailhead	▨	Mangrove
▬▬▬	Pedestrian Walkway	■	Other Location	⚡	Skiing Area	▨	Reef
▤▤▤	Stairs	▲	Campground	⟋	Battlefield	⬚	Swamp

CONVERSION TABLES

°C = (°F - 32) / 1.8
°F = (°C x 1.8) + 32
1 inch = 2.54 centimeters (cm)
1 foot = 0.304 meters (m)
1 yard = 0.914 meters
1 mile = 1.6093 kilometers (km)
1 km = 0.6214 miles
1 fathom = 1.8288 m
1 chain = 20.1168 m
1 furlong = 201.168 m
1 acre = 0.4047 hectares
1 sq km = 100 hectares
1 sq mile = 2.59 square km
1 ounce = 28.35 grams
1 pound = 0.4536 kilograms
1 short ton = 0.90718 metric ton
1 short ton = 2,000 pounds
1 long ton = 1.016 metric tons
1 long ton = 2,240 pounds
1 metric ton = 1,000 kilograms
1 quart = 0.94635 liters
1 US gallon = 3.7854 liters
1 Imperial gallon = 4.5459 liters
1 nautical mile = 1.852 km

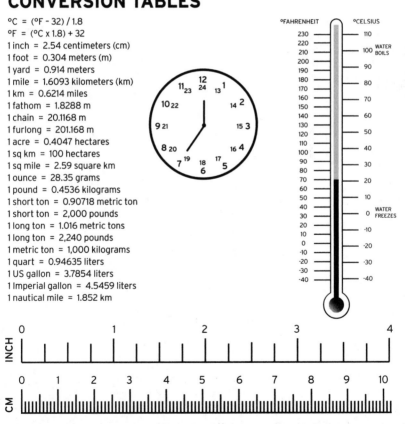

MOON SPOTLIGHT
NORTH CAROLINA COAST
Avalon Travel
a member of the Perseus Books Group
1700 Fourth Street
Berkeley, CA 94710, USA
www.moon.com

Editor: Shaharazade Husain
Series Manager: Kathryn Ettinger
Copy Editor: Michelle Peters
Graphics Coordinator: Elizabeth Jang
Production Coordinator: Elizabeth Jang
Cover Designer: Kathryn Osgood
Cartography Director: Mike Morgenfeld
Map Editor: Brice Ticen
Cartographer: Kat Bennett

ISBN: 978-1-59880-679-3

Front cover photo: bicycle leans against fence on
Bald Head Island beach © iofoto / 123rf.com
Title page photo: porch on Bald Head Island
© iofoto / 123rf.com

Printed in the United States

ABOUT THE AUTHOR

Sarah Bryan

Sarah Bryan was born in North Carolina to a family whose roots reach back through 300 years of Carolina history. Her North Carolina forebears include Moravian pilgrims and Confederate veterans, tugboat pilots and tobacco farmers, preachers and moonshiners.

A third-generation University of North Carolina alum, Sarah grew up in a family filled with Tar Heel pride. There was only one conceivable scenario in which the TV would be turned off during a Tar Heel basketball game: when the score was so close and suspense so high that family elders with weak hearts were in medical danger. There are few things that Sarah loves as much as Tar Heel basketball, but fortunately, many of the close runners-up – including alligators, boiled peanuts, and *The Andy Griffith Show* – are abundantly accessible in North Carolina.

Sarah and her husband Peter Honig live in Durham and are both old-time fiddlers. She works as a folklorist and oral historian at the North Carolina Folklife Institute and is the editor of the *Old-Time Herald*, a long-established magazine about traditional Southern music. Work, music, and hunting for old records carry her to the farthest reaches and remotest crossroads of this huge state. Whether she's at home or on the road, she can be reached at sarahbryan@waccamaw.net.